Essential Trout Flies

DAVE HUGHES

STACKPOLE
BOOKS

To David Detweiler, who has shared the trout waters and the books about them.

Copyright © 2000 by Dave Hughes

Published by
STACKPOLE BOOKS
5067 Ritter Road
Mechanicsburg, PA 17055
www.stackpolebooks.com

Printed in China

First edition

10 9 8 7 6

Cover photo by Jim Schollmeyer
Cover design by Tracy Patterson
Fly box by C&F Design, concept by K Yonenoi

Library of Congress Cataloging-in-Publication Data
Hughes, Dave.
    Essential trout flies / Dave Hughes.
      p. cm.
    Includes bibliographical references (p.   ).
  ISBN 0-8117-2748-3 (pbk.)
        1. Fly tying. 2. Flies, Artificial. I. Title.
  SH451.H775   2000
  688.7'9124—dc21   99-31338
                                          CIP
  ISBN 978-0-8117-2748-8

CONTENTS

CHAPTER 1

Fly Pattern Simplicity

Individual trout patterns are almost all variations on a set of standard themes, called *pattern styles*. The traditional Catskill dry fly is an example. It has been varied endlessly by changing the materials or colors for tails, wings, hackles, and bodies. Each variation has its own name: Adams, Light Cahill, Royal Coachman, Blue-Winged Olive, and so on. But the basic shape of each Catskill style of dry is always the same. So are the steps with which you tie the materials onto the hook.

When you've learned to tie any fly in a style—for example, the Adams in the Catskill style—then you've learned to tie them all. If you think of trout flies in terms of styles, rather than viewing them as a vast scattering of individual patterns, each of which you must patiently— or impatiently—learn to tie, then both your tying and your trout fishing will be greatly simplified. You just need to learn to tie a few styles.

Within each pattern style, a single dressing is usually best known and defines the style. The Catskill drys have their roots on our shores in Theodore Gordon's famous Quill Gordon, which had its own origins in hackled drys that Frederick Halford fished in the last century on British chalkstreams. The Adams is the most famous fly in the Catskill style today and is the most often used because it catches the most trout for the most fly fishers. The Elk Hair Caddis was the first and is now the most famous fly in the elk-hair style, which was invented by the great Montana guide Al Troth. His pattern has been varied both widely and effectively.

If you begin by tying and fishing the single most useful fly in each of a small range of fly styles, you'll be armed with a varied and effective assortment of flies the next time you go fishing. At the same time, you'll be prepared to tie useful variations of those styles when you encounter situations that call for them. Once you've learned to tie the Adams, when a size 16 *Baetis* mayfly hatch appears on your favorite trout stream, you'll already know how to tie a Blue-Winged Olive to match it, because that fly is tied precisely like the Adams.

The Adams is the core fly in the traditional Catskill style of dry flies.

By learning to tie the most important pattern in any fly style, and by being prepared to tie its variations, you can match all of the species in a given insect order. When you've mastered the hackled Catskill dry fly, you can tie a match for any rough-water mayfly species. When you go on to master a single fly in the Sparkle Dun style, you'll be able to tie to a match for any smooth-water mayfly dun. Once you've learned to tie the standard Elk Hair Caddis, you can tie a size and color variation to match any caddis species anywhere in the world.

This applies to searching dry flies as well. When you learn to tie a Royal Wulff, you'll be able to tie any Wulff variation. And it's true for sunk flies as well as for those fished on top. If you can tie a Gold-Ribbed Hare's Ear nymph, you can tie a Dave Whitlock's Fox Squirrel Nymph just as easily. Tie one soft-hackle wet fly, traditional winged wet, or any other style, and you can tie them all. Learn to tie a standard Muddler Minnow, and it takes minor extension of what you've learned to tie the Black Marabou Muddler or any other variation.

I recommend at the outset that you buy two fly boxes, one with open compartments for dry flies, the other with foam inserts in both sides for rows of sunk

Some of the most useful dressings in the Catskill style include the Adams, Light Cahill, Royal Coachman, and Blue-Winged Olive.

With careful fly selection built around the most important flies in each fly style—dry, wet, nymph, and streamer—you can carry just a couple of fly boxes but still catch trout anywhere in the world.

flies: nymphs, wets, and streamers. Don't buy awkward and outsize boxes, but do buy the largest that will fit comfortably in the pockets of whatever you use to carry your fishing gear—a vest, belt bag, chest pack, or creel.

If you fill these two boxes with a somewhat disciplined array of fly styles, chosen for their coverage of a wide range of trout food forms, you'll have a basic set of flies that prepare you to catch trout no matter where in the world you travel to fish. The same two fly boxes also assure your success over the widest range of fishing conditions on your own home waters.

If your flies are chosen right and you fish just a few times a year, these two boxes can contain all the flies you will ever need. After each trip, merely tie to replace what you've lost. You can always grab the boxes and go, knowing you'll rarely arrive at a stream or lakeside without flies that will catch trout.

As you advance as a tier and fisher, these two boxes will still serve as the core of the complex and growing set of fly boxes that most experienced anglers accumulate. My two central fly boxes—one for drys, the other for sunk flies—are often all I take, whether traveling to fish distant waters or fishing my home waters. I know these two boxes contain all the flies I'll need.

As you desire to tie more, I recommend that you build around the two core boxes with two *sets* of fly boxes. The first set of slightly smaller boxes includes a box for hatch-matching drys, another for nymphs based on specific naturals, a third for a wide variety of wet flies, and a fourth for streamers. The second set is for experimental flies. These boxes should be very small. Each holds just those flies, in a variety of styles, that you tie to fish over a specific hatch. I carry a box for the *Baetis,* or blue-winged olives, another for midges, and a third for the western march brown mayflies that hatch heavily on many of my home waters. Most of the flies in these experimental boxes are color and size variations of fly pattern styles listed in this book.

Even if your fly list is already complex, I recommend that you buy two large fly boxes and begin tying a disciplined core of flies to fill them. As you find tying time, fill specific boxes beyond them with hatch-matching drys, imitative nymphs, wet flies, and streamers. Tie into small experimental boxes as you encounter specific hatches repeatedly and discover the need for more than one pattern style to match them. When you tie by pattern style, you'll find that your tying, your trout fishing—and perhaps even your life—become more peaceful and more productive.

Begin by tying the pattern in each style for which the tying steps are shown and described in this book. I've attempted to pick the most useful fly in each style. These few flies can form the core of your simplified fly list. With the resulting fly boxes, you have the right fly in

Always extract your information about trout flies from what you learn while trout fishing.

most fishing situations. If you encounter a situation in which you do not, tie from the lists of variations.

For each dressing listed, the most useful sizes are indicated by boldface type; those are the most common sizes of the natural trout food on which the pattern is based. I recommend that you tie those sizes first and that you tie at least a half dozen of each size. Never tie just two or three of any fly; you'll lose the last one at the instant you discover it has magic against trout. Constructing a half dozen or even a full dozen of any fly also helps you master the steps it takes to tie it.

Your fishing assignment—no book about tying trout flies should be separated from trout fishing—is to tie a core set of flies that cover most trout-fishing situations and take that core of flies fishing. You will discover, as you spend time on the water, your own more central core of favorite flies—the ten to fifteen patterns that you wind up tying to your tippet most often because they catch fish for you almost every time you use them. You can never beat catching trout as a reason to tie a fly.

CHAPTER 2

Tools and Materials

To tie basic trout flies, you need a basic set of tying tools. You can buy these, along with hooks, threads, feathers, and other minor materials you'll need to tie a few flies, in a kit. Most fly-tying kits, however, offer second- or third-rate gear to keep the cost low. The cheaper the kit, the less useful the tools and materials. It's best to buy a few good tools at the outset. You may want to buy a medium- to good-grade kit to get started, however, and then replace the tools one at a time as your expertise increases. But be warned that you'll encounter mild to major frustration using what comes in the kit, and over time you'll replace every item in it with something better.

TOOLS

Vise

A trout-fly vise should have fine, adjustable jaws to securely hold small to medium-size hooks. It should open and close with a knob, lever, or spring-loaded handle that's simple and quick to operate. The stem of the vise should be adjustable for height on a clamp model. Most pedestal models have fixed stems. They must be high enough to place the hook within easy sight and to leave room beneath to turn a thread bobbin around and around the hook.

A clamp vise is best if you are able to set up and tie in a relatively permanent location at a desk, bench, or table. Buy a pedestal model if you travel and want to tie on trips. The vise barrel can be fixed or rotary. A fixed vise holds the hook rigid, and you wrap materials around it. A rotary allows you to turn the hook and to feed materials onto it. I recommend a rotary, though I use it as a fixed. It allows you to reverse the hook, so you can view it from the opposite side, and to turn the hook upside down to tie something to the underside of the fly.

When you buy a vise, buy a materials clip with it, whether it's a spring that goes around the barrel of the vise or a clip that fastens onto it. This holds materials out of the way until you need them.

Scissors

Your tying scissors should be sharp and have straight blades and fine points. The finger holes must be large enough to let you slip them up to the second joint of your ring finger. You'll learn to tie with the scissors constantly in your tying hand. If the finger holes are too small, you'll have to pick them up and set them down every time you cut something. That gets frustrating.

Bobbin and Threader

The bobbin is the most active fly-tying tool. You'll use it for every turn of thread. Buy a good one, with strong legs that you can adjust for tension by bending them in or out. The barrel should be 1 to 2 inches long. I recommend a ceramic bobbin. If you tie a lot, buy four and keep them loaded with the most common colors of thread: black, olive, tan, and gray.

Avoid using a metal bobbin threader to load your thread. It will roughen the mouth of the barrel, which will then fray and cut your thread. The best bobbin threaders I've found are dental floss threaders.

Hackle Pliers

Simple metal hackle pliers work well. Be sure that they are large enough to accommodate the insertion of your index finger. Many have a plastic cover over one tip. Hackle pliers with metal-to-metal contact at the tips often cut hackle stems or break them off. Use fine emery cloth to round the sharp edges and end that problem.

Whip-Finish Tool

I recommend that you start tying with a good whip-finish tool. Later you might graduate to whip-finishing with your fingers, but the tool lets you learn quickly and well, and later gives you the option of the tool over the hand finish. It's quicker to tie a whip finish without picking up the tool, but the tool allows slightly more precise placement of the knot and also reduces the number of times you break off the thread when snugging down the wraps. I prefer the Matarelli tool because it's

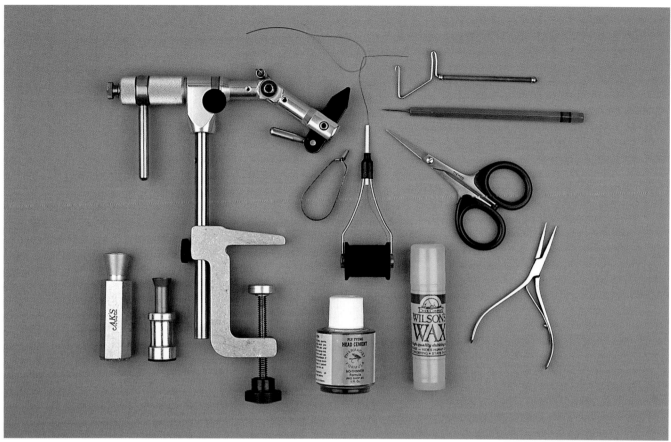

Basic tying tools include: medium and small hair stackers, vise, head cement, dubbing wax, needlenose pliers, hackle pliers, bobbin and threader, scissors, bodkin, and whip-finish tool. JIM SCHOLLMEYER

simple. Whatever brand you choose, you need to carefully follow the instructions that came with it.

Dubbing Wax

At times you'll need a sticky wax to hold fur or synthetic dubbing to your thread. I tie a lot of *flymphs*—rough, wingless wet flies—and fuzzy nymphs. I use wax so often that I tape the lid of my wax container upside down to the stem of my vise. I can lift the tube out, apply wax to the thread, and reinsert the container into its lid. This keeps the wax clean and reduces clutter on my tying bench. Beeswax also works well. Whatever wax you use, smell it before you buy it. You'll use wax most often on sunk flies. If the wax's odor repels trout, you'll always wonder why your luck stinks.

Pliers

Keep a pair of needlenose pliers on your tying bench to debarb hooks before you tie flies on them. If you debarb after you tie, you'll sometimes break a hook and waste all your fly-tying effort.

Hair Stacker

When you cut most hairs—deer, elk, calf, or moose—from the hide, the tips will be uneven and you'll need a hair stacker to align them. You clean all the fuzzy underfur from the butts, place the hair in the stacker barrel, and tap the base on your table a few times. Remove the barrel, and there the tips are, magically even. Begin with a medium-size stacker. Later, as you tie increasingly smaller flies, add a smaller stacker for use on hairs for Comparaduns and other small hatch-matching flies.

Head Cement

One whip finish and a drop of head cement is still the standard way to secure the head of a trout fly. Many tiers, including me, use two whip finishes and dispense with the cement. Head cement is sometimes used on the body of a fly to prevent materials from being cut by the teeth of trout. Whenever you cement the head of a fly, wick any excess out of the eye before it sets by running a hackle tip or stem through the eye. Keep your cement bottle lidded to prevent evaporation and hardening.

Waterproof Pens

Patterns often call for materials that nature fails to provide. For example, many dressings call for grizzly hackle dyed gold or olive. You can purchase an entire dyed neck for $75, or you can buy a $2 marking pen and color the few feathers you need. Get waterproof pens in gold, green, brown, orange, black, and any other required colors.

Waste Container

I keep an old coffee mug on my tying bench to hold waste. Better systems include a frame that suspends an open bag beneath the vise and a special lap waste catcher. With one of these, you can cut things away and not worry about where they fall. That saves the time it takes to deposit each bit of excess into the waste container, but for some reason that doesn't seem to bother me.

Bodkin

A bodkin is simply a needle fixed in a stick of wood. It's useful for applying head cement and also for picking out dubbing to make it rougher after you wrap it onto the hook. You'll find a hundred little uses for a bodkin and should always have one handy on the bench.

Light

A good light is one of the most important tools in any tying setup. It should be bright, shielded to keep the light out of your eyes, and adjustable. I use a 100-watt bulb in a student lamp with a metal arm. The light is lowered over the fly in the vise, directed onto the fly and away from my eyes.

WORK AREA

I tie at a desk with three drawers down each side. One top drawer holds rooster and hen hackle necks, the other tools and hooks that I use almost constantly, kept in open trays. The second level of drawers contains various hairs on one side, feathers on the other. The bottom two drawers hold excess materials that I use less often. Tupperware containers on the desk, always within easy reach, hold various body materials, paired wings, furs, and threads.

One of the most useful storage units I've found recently is a 42-inch-tall Mini-Chest of plastic drawers on wheels. You could easily store a modest trout-tying outfit in one of these. Roll it up to a table, set up the vise, and tie flies. When finished, pack it up and roll it back into a corner. You'll rarely get scolded for clutter.

Whatever type of tyng area you use, cover the surface behind the vise with a sheet of light green artist's mat board. It's easy on the eyes and provides an uncluttered background behind the fly. Keep that area clear of tools, materials, coffee cups, and anything else that might get in the way of the work you're doing and make it more difficult to focus.

MATERIALS

Hooks

Hook Sizes. Hooks in the range of sizes used for trout flies get smaller as their numbers get larger—from size 2, the largest, down to size 28, which is tiny. Only even-numbered hooks are used in today's standard numbering system, though it's possible to buy some hooks in odd-numbered sizes from 13 to 19.

You'll tie streamers and rare nymphs on large size 2 and 4 hooks. Most big trout flies are tied on size 6, 8, and 10 hooks. The average range of dry, nymph, and wet flies are tied on size 12, 14, and 16 hooks, because that's the size range of the most common trout foods imitated with flies. At the small end of the spectrum, you'll use size 18, 20, and 22 flies if you do much hatch matching on smooth water. Flies tied on size 24, 26, and 28 hooks are useful for matching only the tiniest insects when fishing over the most selective trout.

Tying area of the author's fly-tying bench.

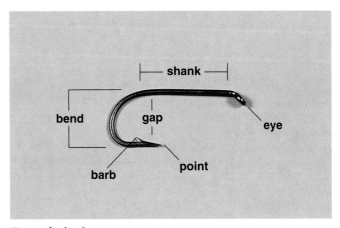

Parts of a hook.

A fly tied on the correct hook style (left) will have proper proportions, which cannot be accomplished if you tie it on a hook too long (right) or too short.

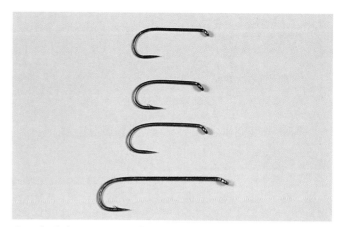

Standard dry, wet, nymph, and streamer hooks (top to bottom), all in size 12.

Trout-Fly Hooks. Hook models are defined by the length of the shank and the diameter of the wire from which they are made. A hook with standard wire and a standard shank length would be about right for a wet fly that you wanted to sink a few inches. Dry flies are tied on light-wire hooks, nymphs on heavy-wire hooks. Streamers are tied on hooks with standard wire but extra long shanks.

The variation from standard is described in Xs. A 1X short hook has a shank the length of a standard hook one size smaller. A 1X long hook has a shank of a hook one size larger. A 1X fine hook is made with wire that would be standard for a hook one size smaller, a 2X fine with wire for a hook two sizes smaller. A 1X stout hook is made with wire standard for one size larger, a 2X stout with wire for a hook two sizes larger. A 1X fine hook is excellent for dry flies; a 2X stout hook is good for wets or nymphs. A 4X fine hook is made to tie dry flies without hackle for flotation. The trade-off is a hook wire too weak to hold a large trout. I no longer use hooks finer than 1X.

Dry-Fly Hooks. The expression *standard dry-fly hook* refers to a hook model with a standard-length shank and 1X fine wire. Examples are the Tiemco 100, Mustad 94840, Dai-Riki 305, and Daiichi 1180.

Nymph Hooks. The *standard nymph hook* is 1X long and 2X stout, though some large nymphs call for 3X or 4X long streamer hooks. Examples of standard nymph hooks are the Tiemco 3761, Mustad 3906B, Dai-Riki 060, and Daiichi 1560. Many nymphs call for *scud hooks,* with a short shank and almost continuous bend from point to eye. Examples include the Tiemco 2487, Mustad 37160, Dai-Riki 135, and Daiichi 1130.

Wet-Fly Hooks. The *standard wet-fly hook* has a standard-length shank made with 2X stout wire. Exam-

ples are the Tiemco 3769, Mustad 3906, Dai-Riki 075, and Daiichi 1530.

Streamer Hooks. The *standard streamer hook* is 3X or 4X long, made with standard wire. Examples are the Tiemco 9300, Mustad 9672, Dai-Riki 700 or 710, and Daiichi 2220. Some streamer styles call for 6X long hooks for very long bodies. These are used most often to imitate long, slender baitfish.

Fur and Synthetic Dubbing Materials

Body dubbing materials can be, and at least at first should be, kept quite simple. You'll want a fine-fibered material that can be rolled tightly to the thread and wrapped into a slender body on the hook. This will be used most often for dry flies. You'll also want a coarse-fibered dubbing that is more loose and fibrous on the hook and when fished in the water. This will be best for nymphs, wets, and streamers. Think of these two needs whenever you buy dubbing materials, and stock a narrow range of colors for each.

Natural Furs. Every fly shop stocks packets of rabbit fur that has been cleaned, bleached, and then dyed in all colors of the spectrum. This fur is excellent. You can twist it tightly to the thread and make a slender body of it, or you can fix it loosely to the thread and create a fuzzy body. Buy it in the most common natural colors, treat it with dry-fly floatant when you want it to float, leave it untreated when you want it to sink, and you will have all the body material you need to tie most trout flies.

Muskrat is excellent for various gray-bodied flies. Squirrel is great for tannish gray. Australian opossum, beaver, red and gray fox, otter, and many other furs are perfect when they come in the colors you desire. If they don't, you can now buy many of them dyed. Angora goat is a rough dubbing with sheen, or brightness, in each

At a minimum, you need two types of dubbing, one fine for dry-fly bodies (left) and one rough for nymph and wet-fly bodies (right).

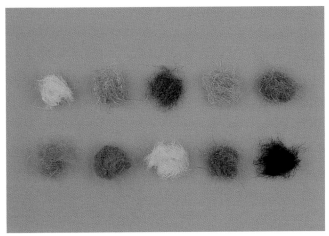

Dubbing furs covering the basic colors: Top row, from left: tan/light cahill; medium brown/hare's ear; dark brown/dark hare's ear; golden brown/golden stone; ginger/cinnamon. Bottom row, from left: light olive/blue-winged olive; bright olive/caddis green; pale yellow/sulfur or pale morning dun; gray/blue dun; black/salmon fly. JIM SCHOLLMEYER

fiber. It can be used by itself for large sunk flies or mixed with rabbit to make it easier to dub for smaller flies. It comes dyed in all colors but is too coarse for most dry-fly bodies.

Synthetic Dubbing. Antron yarn, also known as Sparkle Yarn, is reflective and gives off small flashes when it catches light beneath the surface. It is excellent for wet-fly, nymph, and streamer bodies. You can buy it as yarn, cut it to ⅛- or ¼-inch lengths, toss it into a blender or coffee grinder, and you get a great rough dubbing. It is on the market under a variety of names, in fine enough

form for dry flies as well. It comes in every color you will use and many that you will not.

Many similar synthetics can be purchased under various brand names in a range of colors that covers the color spectrum of natural insects and other trout food forms. If these synthetics have a disadvantage, it is their uniform color. Most natural furs are a mix of colors, as are most natural insects that trout eat.

Blends. To solve the problem of uniformity of color and texture, in both natural and synthetic materials, buy a coffee grinder and mix them. You get the degree of fineness or coarseness you're after, and also a color that is mixed and vibrant rather than monochromatic and bland. By mixing Antron with rabbit fur, for example, you add sparkle to the soft, working fibers of the natural fur.

You can also buy preblends such as Hare-Tron for fine bodies or Hare's Ear Plus for rough bodies. Both come in a range of colors that will cover all your needs. Many other blends are available that provide mixed colors and textures for dry- and sunk-fly bodies.

Dubbing Colors. Natural insects come in a set of repeated color themes that trout see all the time. You'll want to tie most of your flies to reflect that. When you tie within pattern styles, most individual dressings are color variations on the main theme. If you choose a couple of dubbing materials, one fine and the other coarse, and buy each in a range of colors, you'll be able to reach for what you need almost every time you want to tie a trout fly with a dubbed body, which will be most of the time.

If the colors shown in the photo at left don't include what you need, you can often blend two of the colors to get the right shade for a natural insect that you've collected and desire to imitate.

Hackles

Hackles are feathers, generally from the neck of a rooster or hen chicken, tied in by the base or tip, then wound several times around the hook so the fibers flare at 90-degree angles to the shank. Most hackle is wound as a *collar* around the wings or close behind the head of the fly. Sometimes it is *palmered,* wrapped the length of the shank. At other times, hackle fibers are tied on the underside of the hook just behind the head, as a *beard* or *throat.* Hackle usually represents legs and wings of a natural insect. In the case of a dry fly, it also floats the fly.

Rooster Hackle. Dry-fly hackle is taken most often from a rooster neck, or cape. These feathers have fine stems, some reflectance, or *sheen,* and stiff individual fibers of almost equal length as you go up the stem. Dry-fly hackles have little *webbing*—interlocking hairs between the fibers—to absorb water, so they repel it, which is what causes a hackled dry fly to tiptoe on the water. A good rooster neck will have feathers for dry flies from size 8 down to 20, or even 22 or 24. A fine neck enables you to tie trout flies in almost any size.

The denser the feathers on a neck, the better their quality, and the more feathers at the small end, the higher the grade and, as a consequence, the price. You can buy grade 1 necks if you wish, but many experienced and even professional tiers find that grade 2 and 3 necks are the best bargains.

Another excellent bargain is saddle, from the rooster's rump. Saddle feathers are longer than neck feathers but tend to be restricted to a narrow range of sizes. If you tie mostly size 12, 14, and 16 flies, a saddle loaded with feathers in those sizes will serve you well and cost less than a neck of comparable quality. A single feather will tie at least one fly, sometimes two. You'll get more flies of those sizes out of the saddle, but you may not be able to tie the full range of sizes you'd like.

I recommend that you buy four rooster necks to start: brown, medium blue dun, ginger, and grizzly. They will tie most of the flies in this book. Let your budget determine the grade that you get. Don't hesitate to buy half necks. They have enough feathers to propel you well along in your tying life.

Hen Hackle. Hen necks and saddles are better than rooster for wet flies, nymphs, and streamers. The feathers are softer—giving the fly more movement in the water—have more webbing, absorb water, and help sink the fly. And hen neck is much cheaper than rooster.

When buying hen necks, look for long feathers with fibers of equal length along the stem, and also for sheen when you turn the neck under light. The number and quality of feathers in usable sizes will determine the grade of the neck and therefore its price.

You can outfit yourself to tie most of the sunk flies listed in this or any other book with hen necks in brown, medium blue dun, ginger, and grizzly.

Soft Hackle. Many wing and body feathers from birds such as partridge, grouse, starling, and snipe make perfect hackles for wet flies. You'll use them extensively for soft-hackle wets. You can buy these feathers packaged, but you will have a lot of waste and will only get a narrow range of sizes. To get the full range, it's best to buy an entire skin. You'll use partridge most, and it might be all you need, though I recommend a starling skin as well. When choosing a partridge skin, be sure it's been skinned around the neck and head, where the small feathers for size 14, 16, and 18 flies are found.

Hackle: a rooster neck and rooster saddle patch, and a hen neck. JIM SCHOLLMEYER

Rooster neck and hen neck hackle feathers, plus a rooster saddle feather. JIM SCHOLLMEYER

Soft-hackle feathers: brown and gray partridge, grouse wing shoulder feather, and starling back feather.

Turkey tail pair, peacock eye feather, pheasant tail, ostrich, and marabou feathers, plus paired mallard wing feathers. JIM SCHOLLMEYER

Feathers

Many other types of feathers are incorporated into trout flies, in many different ways. You'll need a small selection from the following, some of them in a narrow range of colors.

Turkey. Paired turkey tail feathers, at times called *oak turkey* or *mottled turkey,* are used for Muddler Minnows and wings on hopper and caddis drys. Turkey wing feathers in natural, olive, and pale yellow are used for their *biots*—the short, sharp fibers on the leading edge that can be wound as herl for segmented bodies on small flies. White and light gray *turkey flat feathers,* from the breast and flanks, are perfect for wingposts on parachute drys.

Peacock Eye. Fibers from the peacock eye feather, when wound around the hook shank as herl, form a body that reflects tiny points of light. It's not known why, but almost any fly incorporating peacock herl is a killer. It is used on dry flies, nymphs, wet flies, and streamers.

Pheasant Tail. The center tails from a rooster ring-necked pheasant are reddish brown and well marked. They make excellent tails for wet flies and nymphs. The fibers can be wound as herl to make a slender body that is almost as killing as peacock.

Ostrich. The individual fibers of an ostrich feather can be wound as herl. Ostrich is softer than peacock or pheasant. It absorbs more water and is not useful for dry flies. It is used most often for the thorax or head of a nymph. White and black are called for most often.

Marabou. Soft marabou fluff condenses when wet and undulates in the water. It makes excellent tails and wings on nymphs and streamers. Many nymphs incorporate marabou to give movement and therefore life to the fly. The famous, fish-killing Woolly Bugger style of streamer gets its success from the action of the marabou. Buy it in olive and black; a vest that lacks Olive and Black Woolly Buggers could be said to be empty.

Waterfowl Wings. Primary and secondary feathers from the wings of a mallard are useful for wet- and dry-fly wings, nymph shellbacks, and tent-wings on caddis drys. A pair costs little. Try to buy them matched—a right and left wing from the same bird. When you pluck feathers, keep them paired and matched as well.

Teal primary and secondary feathers are useful in some of the same ways and are better than mallard feathers for tiny no-hackle dry flies. Goose primary feathers have useful biots for tailing nymphs and for bodies of some dry flies.

Wood Duck Flank. Many of the most popular dry flies and wets call for wings of wood duck flank feather. It has a soft yellowish cast that reflects the colors of many natural insects, such as pale morning duns, pale evening

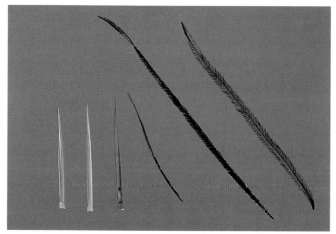

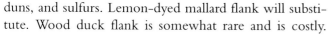

Turkey biots in olive, ginger, and rust, peacock and pheasant herl fibers, and an ostrich herl fiber. JIM SCHOLLMEYER

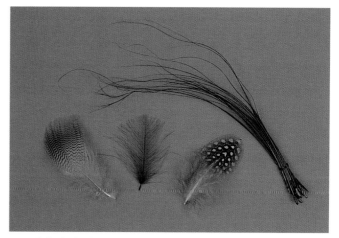

Wood duck flank, CDC, guinea, and dyed hackle feather stems. JIM SCHOLLMEYER

duns, and sulfurs. Lemon-dyed mallard flank will substitute. Wood duck flank is somewhat rare and is costly.

CDC. *Cul-de-canard* feathers, from the preening gland of the duck, have natural oils that cause them to float high. They have been used in Europe for decades but are a recent discovery on this continent. CDC is very effective for dry flies. You should buy it at least in white and blue dun.

Guinea. Breast feathers from guinea fowl are black with white dots, which give legs a segmented or jointed effect. A few nymph dressings call for guinea, and you'll find it handy to have around.

Hackle Feather Stem. The stem of a hackle feather, stripped of its fibers, winds into a slender and ribbed body, excellent for mayfly dun or spinner drys. If you peel away the fibers of a feather that's the color you want, you'll expose the white core of the stem. It's far simpler, and results in more effective flies, to buy stems that have been bleached and dyed to appropriate colors. I recommend pale yellow, olive, and light gray.

Body Hair and Tails

Deer, elk, moose, and calf body hair all find uses as wings, tails, and at times even bodies on dry flies. Spun and clipped hair also forms the head of the Muddler Minnow. Wings and tails for dry flies and streamers are made from calf and squirrel tails. Bucktail, from the white-tailed deer, is useful for wings on streamers.

Deer Hair. Deer body hair is hollow at the core, very light, and floats a dry fly well. It makes perfect wings. When wrapped tightly with thread, it flares at a near-90-degree angle on both sides of the thread. When flared hair is packed tightly and clipped, it makes a compact but bulky head for flies such as Muddlers and hoppers.

Black-tailed deer hair, often sold as coastal deer hair, is fine and finds use as wings on size 14 to 20 dry flies used to imitate caddis, stoneflies, or mayfly duns. Hair from the legs of a deer is fine, not hollow, and has short black tips. It makes the best Compara-dun dry-fly wings.

You will find uses for natural brown and gray deer body hair and for finer coastal deer hair in bleached, natural light, natural dark, and dyed gray. Try to find leg hair in natural light and natural dark.

Elk Hair. Natural tan elk body hair is excellent for many large stonefly and caddisfly drys. Yearling elk is finer and is available in a wide array of dyed colors. It is the perfect material for Elk Hair Caddis wings and also for René Harrop's Hairwing Duns. You'll find yearling elk useful in natural tan, bleached, and light gray.

Moose Body Hair. Moose is a very coarse, almost black hair for tails on dry flies that must float on rough water and survive maulings by many trout. It is standard on such popular patterns as the Royal Wulff. Western tiers often substitute it for hackle fibers on flies, such as the Adams, that they depend upon to float and take trout after trout. Moose body hair finds minor use as wings on a few dry flies and also as the shellback drawn over the thorax of some nymph patterns.

Calf Tail. White calf tail is good for bright, showy dry-fly wings that you can see easily on the water. It's also used as wings on some streamers. It's very difficult to align the tips of calf tail in a stacker. I recommend substituting the less unruly calf body hair for the wings of dry flies in the sizes used most often for trout.

Calf Body Hair. This very fine, bright white hair is straight and much easier to stack than the crinkly calf tail. Calf body hair is easier to work with and makes a neater wing on such flies as the Royal Wulff. Try it wherever a dressing calls for it, and consider substituting it in dressings that call for calf tail.

Deer, elk, moose, and calf body hairs. JIM SCHOLLMEYER

Red and gray squirrel, calf tail, and a natural bucktail.

JIM SCHOLLMEYER

Squirrel Tail. Squirrel tail, both gray and red fox, is useful as winging material on some down-wing dry flies for caddis and stoneflies. It is not compressible, however, and causes a bulky tie-in point. You'll rarely find it called for in trout-fly dressings, though you might find both tails useful to have in your list of fly-tying options.

Bucktail. The flag of a white-tailed deer is brown on the top, white on the underside. The hairs are long and fine and make very good streamer wings. You can buy bucktails dyed any color of the spectrum. I recommend you buy one in its natural colors and use colored waterproof marking pens to dye the little you might need in other colors.

Threads

Size 3/0 nylon is coarse, good only for streamers and some large nymphs. Because of its thickness, it builds up fast on the fly head. You'll have to be conservative with the number of turns you take.

Size 6/0 nylon is much finer, still strong, and the standard for dry flies, wets, and nymphs. It also works well for streamers. If you're going to start with one size of thread, 6/0 is the best.

Size 8/0 nylon is finer than 6/0 and is excellent for small flies but easier to break. As you graduate to smaller flies and at the same time develop a more delicate touch in both your tying and fishing, you might also want to graduate to 8/0 thread. You'll have less thread buildup and tie neater flies.

Pearsall's Gossamer silk is a heavy thread useful for certain soft-hackles, flymphs, and traditional wet flies where the thread color becomes the undercolor to the body. Buy it if you tie a lot of these flies; substitute 6/0 thread if you tie just a few.

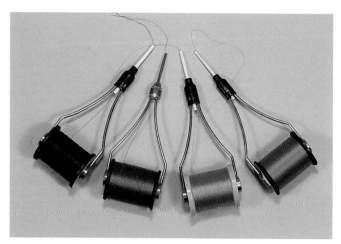

The primary thread colors loaded on bobbins: black, olive, tan, and gray.

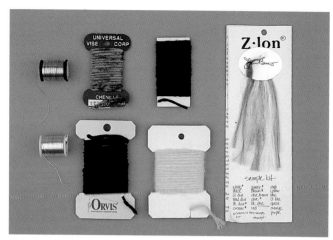

Gold and silver oval tinsel, black and olive chenille, black and gold wool yarns, and a Z-lon sample packet. JIM SCHOLLMEYER

It's best to start with 6/0 in black, tan, olive, and gray. Add other colors and sizes as dressings you wish to tie call for them. If possible, keep each primary thread color loaded on its own bobbin. If you use only one bobbin, you have to switch threads constantly.

Tinsels and Wires

You can buy one spool of flat mylar tinsel, gold on one side and silver on the other, and get by with it for most of your trout-fly tying needs. It should be fine in size, labeled #16/18. Oval tinsels add a slight amount of weight to sunk flies and are better than mylar tinsel for wets, nymphs, and streamers. Buy spools in gold and silver, both colors in small and medium.

Fine wire is usually used as counterwinding over herl to protect the fragile material from the teeth of trout. Many patterns call for wire in copper, gold, and silver, and a few in red and green.

Weighting Wires

You'll need lead wire to wrap around the hook shank for nymphs and some streamers as weight. It comes on spools, the same as thread. The most useful diameters are .010, .015, .020, and .030 inch.

Chenille

Chenille creates round, buggy bodies for sunk flies. It soaks up water and will quickly drown a dry fly. It comes in fine, medium, and large. I recommend all three sizes in black and olive, because they're essential for Woolly Buggers, which are essential to trout fishing. Buy other chenille colors if you discover you need them.

Yarns

Wool yarn is fuzzy and builds up bulk quickly, so it makes good bodies for large streamers and nymphs. It soaks up water and is not used on dry flies. Wool yarn is not used extensively anymore. You can buy it if it's called for in a dressing you want to tie, or substitute rabbit fur dubbing in the appropriate color.

Antron yarn is finer than wool and is water repellent. Individual fibers reflect light beneath the water, hence its common fly-fishing name, Sparkle Yarn. It can be teased out for wings, tied in as trailing shucks on many modern emerger patterns, or chopped short and blended to make dubbing. You'll use Antron yarn most often in gray, amber, olive, and brown.

Floss

I prefer natural silk over rayon floss and recommend starting with red, yellow, and olive. Floss winds flat and makes slender bodies for dry flies and wets. It can also be used for ribbing on larger flies, tags on wet flies, and the bright bodies of some bulky searching dry flies.

Z-lon

This crinkly synthetic fiber is used on some dry flies as wings. It has become the material of choice for imitative applications that call for a trailing shuck in place of the tail on a dry fly. The most useful colors are clear, gray, and amber. You can buy a sample packet that has assorted colors, all in sufficient supply to do a lot of tying. I recommend a sample pack in the subdued colors most useful in trout-fly tying.

BASIC INSTRUCTIONS FOR ALL FLIES

Preparing the Hook

Always pinch the barb down with pliers before tying a fly on a hook. Secure the hook in a vise about midway around the bend, with the shank level. Don't try to cover the point of the hook with the jaws; that crimps the wire, weakening the hook.

Start your thread with two or three turns forward just behind the eye, then five or six turns back over those. Clip the excess thread tag. For most flies, take fairly close thread wraps over the shank, from the eye to the bend. This lays a thread base for all later materials. If you tie on the bare shank, everything will roll around the hook when you're finished. You're now ready to tie in the first material with a *soft loop*. Most flies, though far from all, start with a tail.

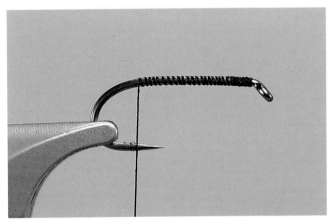

A debarbed hook, with thread started and layered over the shank, ready to begin tying.

Soft Loop

You'll use a soft loop nearly every time you tie a new material to the hook shank—tails, bodies, wings, whatever. The soft loop locks materials on top of the shank, where you want them. If you hold material in place and take the first thread wrap directly around it, you will push it off to the side. Learn the soft loop first, then practice using it every time you tie a fly. (Note that in the following photos, the thumb is held back to allow the thread to show. You would not do this in the process of tying.)

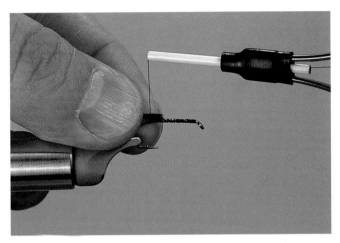

Step 1. Hold the tail material in a tight pinch between your off-hand thumb and forefinger, at the bend of the hook and on top of the shank. Run $1/2$ inch or so of thread up between your forefinger and thumb on the near side of the hook and tail material.

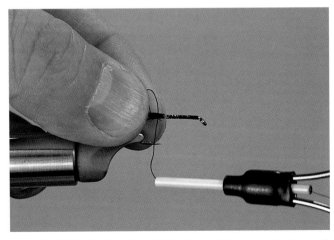

Step 2. Pinch the thread in place, along with the tail, and draw the same length of thread down between your forefinger and thumb on the far side of the hook and the tail. End with a loop pinched above the material and the bobbin directly below the hook.

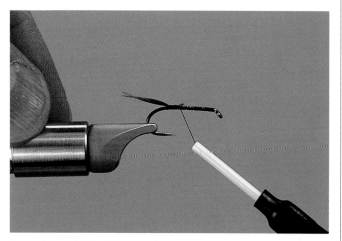

Step 3. Hold the loop tight and use your bobbin to draw it down on top of the tail and hook shank. Pull the bobbin straight down, or even a bit toward you, under the hook shank. When finished, the tail will be locked on top of the hook shank and will not roll off to the side. Take five or six securing turns of thread forward of the soft loop. With practice, you'll begin to hold the soft loop in place, then pop it onto the material with a quick tug on your bobbin.

Whip Finish

You must finish every fly head with a whip finish. Many experienced tiers execute the whip finish with their fingers, eliminating the need for a tool. I recommend that you hold that out as a goal but begin tying with a Matarelli whip-finish tool. It's easier to learn and places the knot more precisely. You will also break your thread less often.

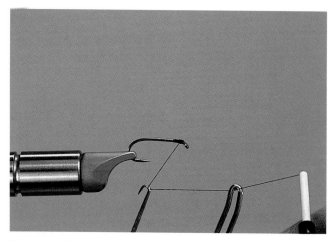

Step 1. Catch the thread from behind with the hook of the tool, about an inch from the hook eye. Slip the thread, again from behind, into the loop in the tool.

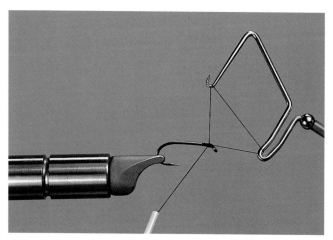

Step 2. Use your bobbin tip to lay the working end of the thread back alongside the hook eye. Roll the tool upward to form a triangle of thread suspended in front of the hook eye.

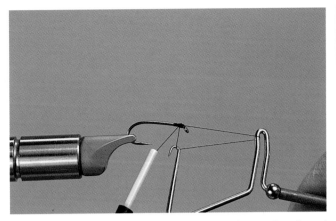

Step 3. Use the hook of the tool to direct the thread while you roll five turns of thread around the head, just behind the hook eye, from the front to the back of the head.

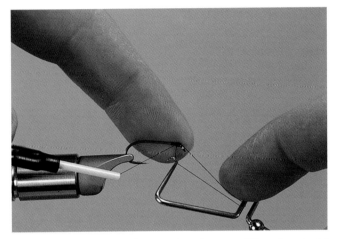

Step 4. Use the forefinger tip of your off hand to hold the thread loops in position. Use the forefinger tip of your tying hand to coax the thread out of the whip-finish tool loop.

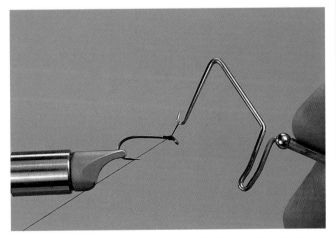

Step 5. Catch the thread loop with the tool hook. Draw the thread tight with the bobbin while directing the thread loop into its final position with the whip-finish tool. Slip the whip-finish hook out of the thread loop, and give a last tug to seat the whip finish.

Cementing the Fly Head

Most tiers apply head cement to the fly as the last step in tying, although some, when using modern prewaxed threads, seat a quick second whip finish and dispense with cement. It's your choice, but do learn to use head cement. It must be liquid enough to penetrate the thread head before drying. I recommend that you tie all your flies for a session, then cement them all at once at the end of the session.

Step 1. Dip your bodkin in the cement. Let a drop run to the bodkin point without falling off. The consistency of your cement will be critical for this—not too thick, not too runny. Place the drop on the thread head of the fly.

Step 2. Before the cement has a chance to dry, run the excess tip or stem of a hackle feather through the hook eye to remove any cement that might dry and block the eye. Be sure that the eye of every fly is clear of both thread and cement before you make the final transfer from the tying bench to your fly box. Little in life is more frustrating than discovering astream that you cannot thread your tippet through the eye of a fly, especially if trout are feeding all around you.

CHAPTER 3

Dry Flies

D ry flies are designed to float on the surface of either moving water or stillwater and to coax trout into striking up to take them. Your goal is to tie them so they float and so trout mistake them for food. Your goal when fishing them, most often, is to present them drifting naturally down the current without drag from your line or leader. More rarely, you'll want to give them the same movement a particular insect might display to feeding trout.

SEARCHING VERSUS IMITATIVE DRY FLIES

Dry flies can be broken roughly into two groups. *Searching drys,* also called attractor or fancy drys, are designed to fish likely holding water and attract trout when they are not feeding in set rise rhythms and no single natural food form is abundant. *Imitative drys* are designed to resemble a particular insect species when it is present in dominating numbers and trout are feeding on it selectively. Observing the right conditions in which to fish either a searching or imitative dry fly can be critical to your fly-fishing success.

Fish searching drys when trout are present and reveal themselves by sporadic rises: one here, another over there, no rise repeated in the same place. Also use them in the absence of rises if the air is warm in spring or fall or cool in the heat of summer, and the water you're fishing is shallow enough that a trout can see something floating by above it. Shallow riffles and runs, 2 to 4 feet deep and a bit bouncy on top, are perfect for searching dry flies, especially when a few insects are out and flying about. Trout will be alert for something adrift on top, but they won't be selective to anything in particular.

Use imitative dry flies whenever trout are feeding visibly on an abundance of a single insect and ignoring everything else. This usually, though not always, happens during a hatch of mayflies or midges, an egg-laying flight of caddisflies, a fall of terrestrial insects, or the presence of enough stoneflies that they're dropping into the water in good numbers along the banks. The two best clues to

Searching dry flies, such as the Royal Humpy on the left, are buggy and very visible. Imitative flies, such as the Pale Morning Hairwing Dun on the right, capture the size, form, and color of a specific species of insect.

When trout feed selectively, it will be to a particular species of insect, such as this pale morning dun mayfly.

selective feeding are the dominance of one insect species and steady, repetitious rises by trout holding in feeding stations.

Materials used to tie a dry fly are selected to repel water; those chosen for a wet fly should absorb water.

When trout are feeding selectively, collect a natural, observe it closely, and select your nearest fly pattern in size, form, and color. Present the fly on the water so that the trout sees it arrive in the same way as the naturals. Usually that means with a drag-free drift.

Selective feeding occurs most often on smooth flats, tailouts, and pools, as well as on lakes and ponds. Imitative flies are typically tied without hackle or with trimmed hackles, because a realistic silhouette of the natural is needed but flotation is not critical. Searching flies, on the other hand, are generally hackled for flotation, as searching fishing is normally done on somewhat rougher water.

Always choose a dry-fly style that will float on the kind of water where you'll cast it. A perfect imitation won't catch many trout if it fails to float and thus doesn't look like anything alive and enticing.

MATERIALS FOR DRY FLIES

Dry flies should always be tied with materials that repel rather than absorb water. Stiff, web-free rooster neck or saddle feathers are best for dry-fly hackles and tails, soft and webby hen or poor-grade rooster for wet flies, nymphs, and streamers. Drys are also tied in shapes that encourage floating rather than sinking. A traditional dry has its hackle collar wound at 90-degree angles to the hook shank; it floats perched on its hackle points. Hackle on a sunk fly is wound so that it sweeps back; it encourages the entry of the fly through the surface as if it were a door to the depths.

With the exception of those tied with CDC feathers, which depend for their flotation on natural oils, dry flies should be dressed with floatant before they are fished. The floatant, usually a spray or paste form of silicone, coats the fibers and repels water. If your dry fly begins to sink after you've fished it for a while, dry it off on a handkerchief, then recoat it with floatant.

DRY-FLY PRESENTATION

It's a slight oversimplification, but three basic presentation types can handle all of your dry-fly fishing. Your goal, again, is that drag-free float. The *upstream cast* is the most common way dry flies are fished. It is most effective with searching flies, on water that is at least somewhat rough. Trout in such water can't see out well and are rarely spooky. But you'll always catch more by taking a position off to one side, rather than directly downstream, then casting upstream and across to the trout at something between a 30- and a 60-degree angle. The line does not fly over the trout in the air and land on their heads. Only the tippet is shown to the trout as the fly floats downstream toward it.

Where the water is smoother and the situation calls for more delicacy, use the *cross-stream reach cast*. Take your position to one side of a lie or a rising trout. Direct your cast to place the fly 2 to 4 feet upstream. As the line loop unfurls in the air, lay your rod over as far as you can reach upstream. The line will then land on the water at an

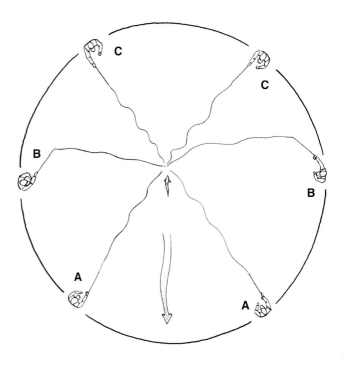

Your presentation depends on the position you've taken relative to the lie of a trout: If you're downstream, use an upstream cast (A); if across from the trout, use the reach cast (B); if upstream, use the downstream wiggle cast (C).

ILLUSTRATION BY RICHARD BUNSE

Your dry fly must be tied so that it floats on the water type where you'll fish it, or it will fail to take any trout.

angle from the rod tip downstream toward the fly. Follow the drift of the fly with your rod, and you extend the free drift of the fly for as much as 10 to 15 feet. Nothing of the line or leader crosses the trout either in the air or on the water.

When trout feed selectively on smooth spring creek or tailwater currents, use the *downstream wiggle cast*. Take your position upstream from visibly feeding trout but at an angle off to the side. Measure your cast with some extra line in the air. As the presentation stroke straightens out toward the trout, wobble the tip of your rod back and forth. The line and leader land with snakelike curves. The fly lands in the feeding lane of the trout. As it floats toward the feeding fish, that slack on the water feeds out and the fly drifts without drag. If the trout refuses, tilt your rod to the side, let the current ease the fly out of the trout's sight, then pick up and cast again.

The upstream cast, reach cast, and wiggle cast can solve almost all of your dry-fly approaches to trout. Learning how to execute these presentations well, then knowing which to use in given currents, will increase your success more than any other single factor in fly fishing.

TRADITIONAL DRY FLIES

Traditional dry flies have hackle fiber tails, slender bodies, upright paired wings, and collars wound from the best rooster hackle. The shape is based on the form of the natural mayfly dun. The hackle represents legs and wings and also floats the fly on fairly rough water. The tail, body, and hackle have the same *footprint* on the water—give the same light impressions—as the natural. That's often more important than an exact imitation of an insect, especially on riffles and runs, where a trout doesn't get a long look at a fly and must make a quick decision to take or refuse.

The Adams is the most important fly in the style to tie and carry in your fly boxes. It was originally tied to represent a flying caddis. The mottled grizzly and brown hackles represent the whirring wings of the natural caddis adult attempting to fly from the water. The dressing takes trout during mayfly and stonefly hatches as well and has become the most popular of all traditional dry flies.

A note about hook sizes: Boldface type in fly recipes indicates the most common sizes of the natural food the pattern imitates and, therefore, the most useful hook sizes.

Adams	
LEN HALLIDAY	
Hook	Standard dry fly, sizes 12, **14, 16,** 18, 20
Thread	Black 6/0 or 8/0
Wings	Hen grizzly hackle tips
Tails	Grizzly and brown hackle fibers, mixed
Body	Muskrat fur dubbing
Hackle	Grizzly and brown

Step 1. Start the thread and layer it over the front third of the hook. Choose two hen hackles, each the width of the hook gap. Pair the feathers back-to-back, measure them the full length of the hook, and peel excess fibers from the lower stems. Use a soft loop and a few turns forward to tie the wings in one-fourth the shank length behind the eye. Use a few thread turns behind the wings to prop them up and a figure eight of thread between them to separate them. Clip the excess wing stems.

Step 2. Layer thread to the bend of the hook. Even the tips of five to ten long, web-free grizzly hackle fibers, and peel or clip them from the stem. Secure them in your hackle pliers. Repeat with the same number of fibers from a brown feather, align them with the tips of the grizzly fibers, and measure them the length of the hook. Use a soft loop and a few turns of thread forward to tie the tails in at the bend of the hook. Wrap the butts forward to about the midpoint of the shank before clipping the excess tail fibers.

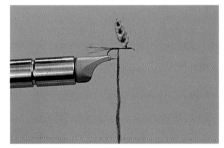

Step 3. Clip a small patch of muskrat fur from the hide. Remove and discard the long guard hairs. Use your forefinger to roll the fur in your palm, mixing it. Use the thumb and forefinger of both hands to spread the fur along the thread, then the thumb and forefinger of your off hand to roll it tightly to the thread, twisting in only one direction. The dubbing skein should be 1 1/2 to 2 inches long, slightly tapered from slender near the hook to fatter at the other end.

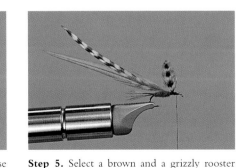

Step 4. Wrap the body forward from the base of the tail to the base of the wing. The body should be slender and tapered. Leave a short gap, about one dubbing turn, between the end of the dubbing and the wings for the hackle. With some practice, you'll work out the correct length and thickness of dubbing skein for each size of fly. That's one reason you tie half a dozen to a dozen of a size at a time.

Step 5. Select a brown and a grizzly rooster neck hackle feather with fibers the length of two hook gaps. The hackle should be just short of the wing tips when wound. Strip all webby fibers from the base of each feather. Pair the feathers with their curved sides together. Tie them in, concave sides facing you, with the stems between the wings. Take two turns of thread behind the wings, pinch the wing tips together and tug them upright, and take five to six turns of thread in front of the wings. Clip the excess stems.

Step 6. Grasp the tip of the far hackle with your hackle pliers. Wind two to three turns behind the wings, three to four more toward the hook eye in front of the wings, leaving room for the head. Tie off the hackle with three to four turns of thread, and clip the excess tip. Wind the second hackle through the first. Tie it off and clip the tip. Gather all hackle fibers back from the eye with your off hand, and take a few turns of thread to hold the hackle back and to form an even base for the head. Whip-finish the fly, clip the thread, and cement the head.

Useful Variations

These variations cover the most common colors of natural mayfly duns. The Light Cahill imitates eastern sulfurs and western pale morning duns. The Blue-Winged Olive represents the widest array of hatches, all across the continent. The Blue Dun represents many gray mayflies. The March Brown and Dark Hendrickson represent specific eastern mayflies, but also look like many other naturals that show themselves to trout in brown and dark gray. The Royal Coachman is an excellent searching dry fly.

For your simplified dry-fly box, I recommend the Adams and Light Cahill in sizes 12, 14, and 16, because they give you a dark and a light option. If you decide to use this traditional style to imitate a hatch, try the Blue-Winged Olive or any other listing that represents the hatch on water where you need hackle for flotation. For hatches on smooth water, consider one of the more imitative styles, such as the Hairwing Dun or Sparkle Dun.

| 1 | 2 | 3 |
| 4 | 5 | 6 |

1	Blue-Winged Olive
Hook	Standard dry fly, sizes 12, **14, 16,** 18, 20
Thread	Olive 6/0 or 8/0
Wings	Blue dun hen hackle tips
Tails	Blue dun hackle fibers
Body	Olive fur or synthetic dubbing
Hackle	Blue dun

2	Blue Dun
Hook	Standard dry fly, sizes 10, **12, 14,** 16, 18
Thread	Gray 6/0 or 8/0
Wings	Medium blue dun hen hackle tips
Tails	Medium blue dun hackle fibers
Body	Muskrat fur
Hackle	Medium blue dun

3	Light Cahill
Hook	Standard dry fly, sizes 12, **14, 16,** 18
Thread	Tan 6/0 or 8/0
Wings	Wood duck flank fibers, upright and divided
Tails	Ginger hackle fibers
Body	Cream fur or synthetic dubbing
Hackle	Ginger

4	March Brown
Hook	Standard dry fly, sizes 10, **12, 14,** 16
Thread	Orange 6/0 or 8/0
Wings	Wood duck flank fibers, upright and divided
Tails	Ginger hackle fibers
Body	Tan fur or synthetic dubbing
Hackle	Ginger and grizzly

5	Dark Hendrickson
Hook	Standard dry fly, sizes **12, 14,** 16, 18
Thread	Gray 6/0 or 8/0
Wings	Wood duck flank fibers, upright and divided
Tails	Dark blue dun hackle fibers
Body	Muskrat fur
Hackle	Dark blue dun

6	Royal Coachman
Hook	Standard dry fly, sizes **12, 14,** 16, 18
Thread	Black 6/0 or 8/0
Wings	White mallard feather sections, upright and divided
Tails	Golden pheasant tippet
Body	Peacock herl, red floss, peacock herl
Hackle	Dark brown

Fishing Notes

Traditional dry flies float well if treated with dry-fly floatant, always best used before fishing the fly. Whenever you encounter a hatch of mayflies on somewhat rough water—anything but a spring creek or tailwater flat—capture a natural and try the traditional dry that's closest to it in size and color. If no hatch is happening, try the Adams, Light Cahill, or even Royal Coachman as a searching dressing—the drab Adams if you can see it, a brighter fly if you cannot.

Fish these hackled dry flies on upstream casts tight to visible rising trout or with a series of casts that float the fly over all the possible lies in what you read to be good holding water. The rougher the water, the closer you should wade and the shorter you should cast so you can see the fly, follow its drift, and notice when a trout takes it. Watch out for drag caused by currents tugging at your leader and line. If the fly moves unnaturally, lift it off and cast again. If a fish hits, lift your rod tip quickly but gently to set the hook.

Catskill-style dry flies are most useful where the water is at least slightly rough on top, though they'll often take trout where the water is smooth.

HAIRWING DUNS

René Harrop developed his Hairwing Duns as mayfly imitations in the late 1980s. The style shows trout a wing silhouette that is held upright but slanted back, like the natural but unlike most mayfly dun imitations, the wings of which stand straight or even tilt forward. The style is also versatile. The hackle is clipped on the bottom, so the fly floats flush in the surface film and is imitative of the mayfly shape on smooth pools and flats. But its hackle and hairwing keep it afloat on rougher water, making it an excellent design for fishing riffles and runs as well.

If you enjoy matching hatches but desire to tie only one mayfly dun style, this would be a good one. The listed Olive Hairwing Dun imitates tiny little olives, large green drakes, and many famous blue-winged olive hatches in between. *Field & Stream* once polled its writers: "If you could fish with just one fly, which would it be?" This was mine. It is useful in the full range of sizes.

Olive Hairwing Dun
RENÉ HARROP

Hook	Standard dry fly, sizes **12, 14, 16, 18, 20**
Thread	Olive 6/0 or 8/0
Tails	Blue dun hackle fibers, split
Body	Olive fur or synthetic
Hackle	Blue dun
Wing	Gray dyed yearling elk or coastal deer hair

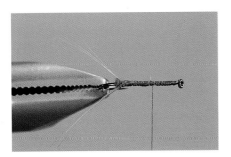

Step 1. Start the thread, layer the shank, and clip excess. Twist a tiny amount of dubbing to the thread, and make a small knot of fur at the bend of the hook. Select two to four web-free tailing fibers from a feather at the side of a rooster neck. These are called *spade feathers.* Pull or clip the fibers from the hackle stem with their tips aligned. Measure them the length of the hook. Use a soft loop to tie them in on the far side of the dubbing knot. Repeat on the near side. The knot will flare the fibers at 45-degree angles to the hook shank.

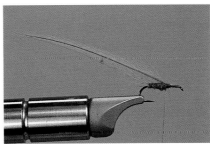

Step 2. Twist enough dubbing to the thread to make a slender body over the rear half of the hook shank. Wind it to the midpoint of the hook. It should be slender and slightly tapered. Select a hackle feather with fibers one and a half to two times as long as the hook gap. Strip the webby fibers from the lower stem, and tie in the feather by the stem at the end of the body. Clip the excess stem.

Step 3. Twist enough dubbing to the thread to finish the body to the hook eye. This represents the thorax region of the mayfly and should be fatter than the back half, tapering down to the hook eye. Wrap five evenly spaced turns of hackle forward over this thorax. Tie off the hackle tip and clip the excess tip behind the hook eye. You can also break the tip off by twitching your hackle pliers back, cutting the hackle stem on the thread wraps that hold it in place. This is quicker.

Step 4. Clip a small patch of deer or elk hair from the hide. Only experience—tying by the dozen—will tell you the precise amount of hair to cut for each size of fly. Clean all fuzzy under-fur from the hair butts, and align the tips of the hair in your stacker. Remove the hair from the stacker, hold it by the butts in your tying hand, and measure it from the hook eye to the bend—the length of just the hook shank. The wing should stand up, with its tips straight above the end of the body.

Step 5. Shift your grip on the wing hair to your off hand, and hold it tightly on top of the hook shank. Use a soft loop to secure the hair in place just behind the hook eye. Take eight to ten more turns of thread, working from the first turn back over the wing, while holding the wing hair out of the way. These thread wraps form a gap between the flared wing hairs and the flared hair butts. Capture and hold the wing butts back from the hook eye, and place one or two whip finishes behind the eye. Clip the thread.

Step 6. Gather the hair butts with your off-hand fingers, and clip the butts straight across just in front of the hook eye. Clip a V-notch out of the bottom of the hackle, leaving a bit more than 180 degrees of the hackle arc. This serves both to support the fly and to represent the legs of a floating natural. To clip this V-notch, remove the fly from the vise and hold it upside down by the wing. If you have a rotary vise, invert the fly and make the single cut.

Useful Variations

As with the earlier traditional dressings, the most useful variations of René Harrop's Hairwing Dun style represent the most common sizes and colors of natural mayfly duns. The Pale Morning Hairwing Dun represents the western PMD hatch as well as eastern sulfurs. The Cream and Mahogany variations imitate tan and brown species, such as the march brown. The Blue Dun and Slate Hairwing Duns are useful over a wide variety of hatches. The Black & White Hairwing Dun imitates tiny Trico (*Tricorythodes*) mayflies and is easy to see on the water despite its small size.

The listed variations will fish for the full range of mayfly hatches, wherever you might encounter them. I recommend that you tie the Olive and Pale Morning versions, in sizes 12 through 18, for your basic dry-fly box.

1	2	3
4	5	6

1	Pale Morning Hairwing Dun	2	Cream Hairwing Dun	3	Mahogany Hairwing Dun
	RENÉ HARROP		RENÉ HARROP		RENÉ HARROP
Hook	Standard dry fly, sizes **14, 16,** 18	Hook	Standard dry fly, sizes 12, **14, 16,** 18	Hook	Standard dry fly, sizes 10, **12, 14,** 16
Thread	Pale yellow 6/0 or 8/0	Thread	Tan 6/0 or 8/0	Thread	Brown 6/0 or 8/0
Tails	Ginger hackle fibers, split	Tails	Ginger hackle fibers, split	Tails	Brown hackle fibers, split
Body	Pale yellow-olive fur or synthetic	Body	Cream fur or synthetic	Body	Cinnamon fur or synthetic
Hackle	Ginger	Hackle	Ginger	Hackle	Brown
Wing	Bleached yearling elk or coastal deer hair	Wing	Natural yearling elk or bleached coastal deer hair	Wing	Brown yearling elk or coastal deer hair

4	Blue Dun Hairwing Dun	5	Slate Hairwing Dun	6	Black & White Hairwing Dun
	RENÉ HARROP		RENÉ HARROP		RENÉ HARROP
Hook	Standard dry fly, sizes 12, **14, 16,** 18	Hook	Standard dry fly, sizes **12,** 14, 16, 18	Hook	Standard dry fly, sizes 18, **20, 22,** 24
Thread	Gray 6/0 or 8/0	Thread	Iron gray or black 6/0 or 8/0	Thread	Black 8/0
Tails	Light blue dun hackle fibers, split	Tails	Dark blue dun hackle fibers, split	Tails	Dark blue dun or black hackle fibers, split
Body	Muskrat belly fur or light gray synthetic	Body	Muskrat back fur or dark gray synthetic	Body	Black fur or synthetic
Hackle	Grizzly	Hackle	Dark blue dun	Hackle	Dark blue dun or black
Wing	Light gray dyed yearling elk or coastal deer hair	Wing	Slate gray yearling elk or coastal deer hair	Wing	Bleached yearling elk or coastal deer hair

Fishing Notes

Hairwing Duns are unusual in that they can be used as mayfly dun imitations on smooth water and also on water that is at least somewhat rough. I use them most often for what I term *presentation fishing*—fishing delicate tackle and fragile tippets over selectively rising trout on smooth flats or on lakes and ponds. This kind of fishing calls for 3- to 5-weight rods, 12- to 15-foot leaders with 5X, 6X, or even 7X tippets at least 3 feet long, and flies usually size 16 and smaller.

For rougher water, riffles, and runs, the same rods are useful, but the leaders should be just 10 to 12 feet long, with 4X and 5X tippets. Flies are most often sizes 12 and 14. Hairwing Duns will often serve you well when no hatch is happening but trout are willing to rise to drys. When used as searching flies, the bright Pale Morning Hairwing Dun will serve you best because you can see it easily.

In all of your trout fishing, if trout refuse the bright version, switch to a darker one and see if they'll accept that.

Hairwing Duns work well where the water is smooth and trout are selective, but they also float well and fool fish on the slightly rough water of gentle riffles and runs.

SPARKLE DUNS

The Sparkle Dun style was developed by John Juracek and Craig Mathews of Blue Ribbon Flies in West Yellowstone, Montana. It's an emerger modification of Al Caucci and Bob Nastasi's Compara-dun style for mayfly duns, which is a change worked on Fran Better's original Haystack. All have deer-hair wings flared in a 160-degree arc over the body and lack hackles. The Haystack has a deer-hair tail. The Compara-dun has split hackle fiber tails. The Sparkle Dun has a Z-lon fiber tail to represent the shuck of the nymph trailing off the back of the body of the emerging dun.

A Sparkle Dun floats flush in the surface film and represents an emerging mayfly dun trapped helplessly in its own nymphal exoskeleton. The style is very important if you fish over small mayfly hatches on smooth water. A Sparkle Dun in the appropriate size and color is my first choice when picky trout are working a spring creek or tail-water mayfly emergence.

Wing hair for Sparkle Duns, often called Compara-dun hair, is fine, either solid or at most slightly hollow, with short black tips. The best comes from the leg of a deer. You can use natural or dyed coastal deer hair or yearling elk if the tips are not too long.

Light Olive Sparkle Dun

JURACEK AND MATHEWS

Hook	Standard dry fly, sizes 14, 16, **18, 20**, 22
Thread	Olive 6/0 or 8/0
Wing	Light gray dyed deer or yearling elk hair
Tail	Pale gray Z-lon fibers
Body	Light olive Antron or fur dubbing

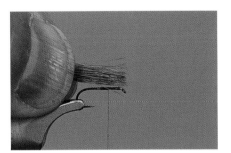

Step 1. Debarb the hook, fix it in the vise, and layer thread over the front half of the shank. Return the thread to a point one-third the length of the shank behind the eye. Select fine deer hair with very short black tips. Clip a small patch from the hide, remove all underfur and short hairs, and align the tips in your stacker. Remove the hair from the stacker, hold it in your off hand, and measure it the length of the hook shank, including the eye.

Step 2. Pinch the wing hair firmly over the tie-in point, one-third the shank length behind the eye, and secure it there with a soft loop drawn down tight over the hair. Take eight to twelve more tight turns over the hair butts, toward the rear of the hook, without releasing your grip on the butts. Raise the butts from the shank, and slip your scissors in to cut the butts at a slant so that when wrapped down with thread, they will form a tapered base for the front of the body.

Step 3. Layer thread over the wing butts and continue to the bend of the hook. Clip several Z-lon fibers from the skein, and measure them the length of the hook shank. Hold them on top of the hook shank at the bend, and tie them in with a soft loop. Take thread wraps forward over the Z-lon butts, to merge with the wing butts, before clipping the excess Z-lon. This forms an even base for the body of the fly.

Step 4. Twist Antron or fur dubbing tightly to the thread. Wind it forward from the base of the tail to the base of the wing to form the body. It should be slender at the back and taper slightly to fatter at the front. The natural mayfly dun has a slender but tapered body.

Step 5. Separate the rear third of the wing fibers and draw them back with your off hand, forming a gap between the rear third and the front two-thirds. Take a single turn of thread through this gap and seat it tightly to the hook shank. This is critical to hold the wing upright later when the fly is fished. Draw the second third of hair back, and take a turn between the back two-thirds and the front third. Hold all of the hair firmly back and take many turns of thread tight against the front, forming a *thread dam* to prop the wing upright.

Step 6. Add a small amount of dubbing to the thread. Take the first turns of dubbing braced tight against the wing, the rest tapering down to the eye. Form a neat thread head behind the eye, whip-finish the head, clip the thread, and apply head cement. Tease the wing into a neat 160-degree arc over the hook shank. Remove the fly from the vise, or turn it upside down if you use a rotary. Clip any stray hair fibers that violate the tidy arch of the wing.

Useful Variations

	1	2	3
	4	5	6

The Light Olive Sparkle Dun matches prolific little olive *(Baetis)* and blue-winged olive hatches. The Pale Morning Sparkle Dun matches abundant PMD, pale evening dun, and sulfur hatches. Begin with those two, and expand your list as you encounter other hatches. The listed Sparkle Duns represent the most common colors in mayfly hatches.

It might seem redundant to carry traditional dressings, Hairwing Duns, and Sparkle Duns all in the same sizes and colors to match the same hatch, but that is far from true. Different patterns fish best over different water types, from rough to smooth. Even on the same water, trout will at one time want one style, and the next day, hour, or even moment refuse it. Some trout in a pod will focus on duns, others on emergers. The more options you carry for a given hatch, the more situations you'll solve, and therefore the more trout you'll catch.

1	Tan Sparkle Dun
	JURACEK AND MATHEWS
Hook	Standard dry fly, sizes **12**, **14**, 16, 18
Thread	Black 6/0 or 8/0
Wing	Tan deer or yearling elk hair
Tail	Gray Z-lon fibers
Body	Tannish gray Antron or fur dubbing

2	Pale Morning Sparkle Dun
	JURACEK AND MATHEWS
Hook	Standard dry fly, sizes 14, **16**, **18**, 20
Thread	Pale yellow 6/0 or 8/0
Wing	Bleached deer or yearling elk hair
Tail	Pale gray Z-lon fibers
Body	Pale yellow-olive Antron or fur dubbing

3	Cream Sparkle Dun
	JURACEK AND MATHEWS
Hook	Standard dry fly, sizes 14, 16, **18**, **20**
Thread	Tan 6/0 or 8/0
Wing	Natural light deer or yearling elk hair
Tail	Pale gray Z-lon fibers
Body	Creamish tan Antron or fur dubbing

4	Mahogany Sparkle Dun
	JURACEK AND MATHEWS
Hook	Standard dry fly, sizes 12, **14**, **16**, 18
Thread	Brown 6/0 or 8/0
Wing	Brown deer or yearling elk hair
Tail	Brown Z-lon fibers
Body	Brown Antron or cinnamon fur dubbing

5	Dark Olive Sparkle Dun
	JURACEK AND MATHEWS
Hook	Standard dry fly, sizes 14, **16**, **18**, 20
Thread	Olive 6/0 or 8/0
Wing	Dark gray dyed deer or yearling elk hair
Tail	Olive Z-lon fibers
Body	Dark olive Antron or fur dubbing

6	Black & White Sparkle Dun
	JURACEK AND MATHEWS
Hook	Standard dry fly, sizes 16, 18, **20**, **22**
Thread	Black 6/0 or 8/0
Wing	Bleached deer or yearling elk hair
Tail	Gray Z-lon fibers
Body	Black Antron or fur dubbing

Fishing Notes

Sparkle Duns are tied to represent emerging mayflies. You find trout feeding on emergers most often in smooth water, pools and flats, because the surface film is a barrier on unbroken water, and that is where most natural insects get stuck in their shucks. In rough water, the surface film is broken by its own agitation. Emerging insects move through it without getting stuck, though they might encounter difficulty floating once they've done it.

Emergence problems occur most often in small insect species, because the surface film is a barrier to them, whereas larger insects use their mass to break right through. Mayflies and midges size 16 and smaller often get stuck in the film and in their shucks on smooth water. Insects size 14 and larger rarely get stuck, whether the water is riffled or still.

You'll find the Sparkle Dun style most useful in size 16 and smaller, when presented to rising trout on very smooth water or cast to trout feeding selectively on tiny insects. The cross-stream reach cast and downstream wiggle cast are essential methods when you fish these tiny flies on the water types where they're most effective.

Sparkle Duns are most effective when you're matching hatches of small insects on smooth water, a combination that often produces excellent emerger fishing.

THORAX DUNS

Thorax Duns were originated by Vincent C. Marinaro for the selective trout on Pennsylvania limestone streams and recorded in his *A Modern Dry-Fly Code* (Crown, 1950). They were modified in the 1980s by Mike Lawson, fly-shop owner on the Henrys Fork of the Snake River in Idaho. The original style had hen hackle tip wings set well back on the body. Two hackles were wound at a tilt, surrounding the wings. The current style uses turkey flat feathers for wings. One high-grade hackle is wound in several turns spread over the thorax of the fly.

The Thorax Dun is one of the most attractive mayfly dun styles you can tie, and also one of the most imitative. A few sizes and colors in your fly boxes give you an excellent set of options whenever you fish over trout feeding selectively on duns in smooth currents.

White turkey flat can be substituted for the darker wing on any Thorax Dun variation to make the fly more visible, though it will be less imitative.

Pale Morning Thorax Dun	
Hook	Standard dry fly, sizes **14**, **16**, 18, 20
Thread	Pale yellow 6/0 or 8/0
Wing	Light gray turkey flat
Tails	Ginger hackle fibers, split
Body	Pale yellow-olive fur or synthetic dubbing
Hackle	Ginger, wound over thorax and clipped on bottom

Step 1. Debarb the hook and fix it in the vise. Start the thread and layer it over the front half of the hook shank. Prepare a turkey flat feather by peeling away all fibers that do not line up straight across the top of the feather. Select and separate a section of the flat feather ¼ to ½ inch across, depending on the size of fly you're tying.

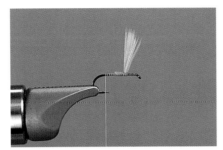

Step 2. Clip the wing section from the turkey flat feather, being sure the tips are aligned. Gather the wing by the base in the thumb and forefinger of your off hand, measure it the length of the entire hook, and tie it in one-third the length of the shank behind the eye, with the tips over the hook eye. Hold the wing upright and take enough turns of thread directly in front to form a *thread dam* that holds the wing straight up. Clip the excess wing butts and layer thread over them to the hook bend.

Step 3. Dub a tiny knot of fur at the hook bend. Select two to four hackle fibers from a web-free spade feather at the side of a rooster neck. Cut or peel the fibers from the hackle stem, with their tips aligned. Measure them the length of the hook—the same length as the wing—and tie them in on the near side of the hook. Repeat on the far side with two to four more fibers the same length. Wrap thread over them back against the fur knot until they are split at 45-degree angles to the hook shank.

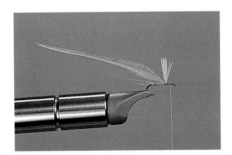

Step 4. Twist dubbing to the thread and wrap a slender abdomen forward to the base of the wing, leaving a slight gap just behind the wing. Select a high-quality hackle feather with fibers the length of the hook shank, or two hook gaps. The hackle when wound should be just shorter than the wing. Peel webby fibers from the base of the feather. Tie it in with two or three tight thread wraps over the stem in the gap between body and wing, and with five or six more wraps ahead of the wing. Clip the excess stem.

Step 5. The thread is now in front of the wing, just behind the hook eye. Twist the same amount of dubbing to the thread that you used for the abdomen, in a slender skein. Wrap this dubbing back to the wing, cross under it, and fill the gap behind the wing. Wrap dubbing forward, crossing under the wing again, and tapering it down to the hook eye. The thorax on this style of fly should be thicker than the slender abdomen.

Step 6. Wind the hackle forward in evenly spaced turns, taking three or four behind the wing and four to five in front. Tie it off at the hook eye and clip the excess stem. Form a neat thread head, whip-finish, clip the thread, and cement the head. Remove the fly from the vise, and hold it upside down or use your rotary to invert it. Clip the hackle in a V-notch on the bottom so that it's just more than a 180-degree arc over the hook shank.

Useful Variations

The most useful Thorax Duns are imitative of the color themes repeated during mayfly hatches. The pale morning dun in the West and various sulfurs in the East are among the most common, which is why that dressing is listed as the basic. Trout will often take such a bright fly in the right size, even when the color is quite wrong for the insect on the water.

The many little olives *(Baetis),* both East and West, along with abundant blue-winged olives *(Ephemerella)* and green drakes *(Drunella),* make a drabber olive version of the fly next in importance. With these two colors, you can cover most hatches you'll encounter. Add color variations as you discover hatches that call for them.

If you plan to keep your fly boxes absolutely basic, you might choose to use other dressing styles, such as the Catskills on rough water and Sparkle Duns on smooth water, to match mayfly hatches. The Thorax Duns, however, seem to always sit on the water with the precise posture of the naturals. That posture is often the key to successful imitation. If you get into

mayfly hatches that seem difficult to solve, try this style and see if a few of its variations don't ease their way onto your basic list and into your basic dry-fly box.

1	2	3
4	5	6

1	Light Olive Thorax Dun
Hook	Standard dry fly, sizes 14, **16, 18**, 20
Thread	Olive 6/0 or 8/0
Wing	Pale gray turkey flat
Tails	Light blue dun hackle fibers, split
Body	Light olive fur or synthetic dubbing
Hackle	Light blue dun, wound over thorax and clipped on bottom

2	Dark Olive Thorax Dun
Hook	Standard dry fly, sizes 14, 16, **18, 20**
Thread	Olive 6/0 or 8/0
Wing	Dark gray turkey flat
Tails	Dark blue dun hackle fibers, split
Body	Dark olive fur or synthetic dubbing
Hackle	Dark blue dun, wound over thorax and clipped on bottom

3	Callibaetis Thorax Dun
Hook	Standard dry fly, sizes **12, 14**, 16, 18
Thread	Cream 6/0 or 8/0
Wing	Gray speckled partridge breast
Tails	Grizzly hackle fibers, split
Body	Creamish gray fur or synthetic dubbing
Hackle	Grizzly, wound over thorax and clipped on bottom

4	Mahogany Thorax Dun
Hook	Standard dry fly, sizes 12, **14, 16**, 18
Thread	Brown 6/0 or 8/0
Wing	Dark gray turkey flat
Tails	Brown hackle fibers, split
Body	Cinnamon fur or synthetic dubbing
Hackle	Brown, wound over thorax and clipped on bottom

5	Slate Thorax Dun
Hook	Standard dry fly, sizes 12, **14, 16**, 18
Thread	Gray 6/0 or 8/0
Wing	Gray turkey flat
Tails	Dark blue dun hackle fibers, split
Body	Muskrat fur or gray synthetic dubbing
Hackle	Dark blue dun, wound over thorax and clipped on bottom

6	Black & White Thorax Dun
Hook	Standard dry fly, sizes 18, **20, 22**, 24
Thread	Black 6/0 or 8/0
Wing	White turkey flat
Tails	Grizzly hackle fibers, split
Body	Black fur or synthetic dubbing
Hackle	Grizzly, wound over thorax and clipped on bottom

Fishing Notes

Because it has hackles and fairly supportive tails, the Thorax Dun style will float and fish well enough that you should not discount it for hatches in riffles and runs. However, the style is designed for the smooth water of spring creeks and tailwaters and is most effective where the water is flat. Because the hackle is clipped from the bottom, the fly rides with its body flush in the surface film. That shows the trout a perfect silhouette, similar to that of a natural mayfly dun. It also lowers the profile of the fly and makes it harder for you to see on rough water, even though it might float well enough.

If the Thorax Dun will float and you are able to follow that float to notice takes, the style is excellent wherever you encounter selective trout. Fish the style with delicate tackle and long, fine tippets. Use the presentation method—upstream, reach cast, or wiggle cast—most suited to the type of water you're fishing.

When you're imitating mayflies such as this pale morning dun, consider the Thorax Dun style if trout refuse other imitations.

SPENTWING SPINNERS

Mayfly spinner falls, the last collapse of egg-laying females, can be almost impossible to figure out, yet they're easy to solve once you realize what is happening and switch to the right fly. Natural spinners are nearly invisible once they land on the water. You see rises, usually in the low light of evening, but have no idea what the trout are taking. Often those trout are sipping spent spinners. Get your nose right next to the water so you can see them, or suspend an aquarium net in the surface currents to collect them.

I recommend that you carry at least the Red Quill Spinner and Pale Morning Biot Spinner to solve most spinner situations. The Red Quill matches the final stage of many mayflies that are called mahoganies in the dun stage, as well as western green drakes and some eastern blue-winged olives, which are also brownish red in the spinner stage. The Pale Morning Biot Spinner imitates many pale morning dun, pale evening dun, and sulfur spinners. It is more visible than other spinner dressings. Use it when size is more important than color, and you can get away with a slight mismatch, if some other color of spinner is falling to the water.

Red Quill Spinner

Hook	Standard dry fly, sizes 12, **14**, **16**, 18
Thread	Brown 6/0 or 8/0
Tails	Brown hackle fibers, split
Body	Reddish brown dyed hackle stem
Wings	Brown hen hackle tips
Hackle	Brown, clipped top and bottom

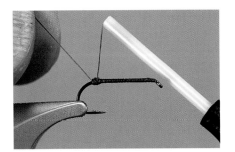

Step 1. Debarb the hook, secure it in the vise, and layer thread from the eye to the bend. Make a slight thread lump there by holding the unclipped tag end of the thread up and taking ten to fifteen turns of thread back and forth against it and just in front of it. This can be done without the thread tag by crisscrossing turns of thread at the bend. You can also use a tiny dubbing knot, as you did to split the tails on earlier dun dressings. Use fur or synthetic the same color as the body you'll use.

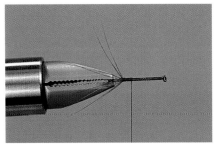

Step 2. Select six to ten web-free hackle fibers, peel or cut them from the hackle stem, and measure them the length of the entire hook—eye, bend, and all. The tails on a spinner should be overlength. Hold them in position above the bend with a pinch, and tie them in just in front of the thread lump. Take several turns of thread back to the lump, at the same time using your off-hand fingers to splay the fibers wide. You can leave them splayed, which supports the fly better, or cut out those in the center, forming more imitative split tails, after you've finished the fly.

Step 3. Clip a presoaked hackle stem an inch or two back from the fragile tip: the smaller the hook, the thinner the part of the stem where you want to tie it in, for proper segmentation. Tie in the stem by the tip one-third the hook shank length behind the eye. Wrap thread to the base of the tail and back to the tie-in point to form an even underbody for the hackle stem. Wrap the stem forward over two-thirds of the hook shank, tie it off, and clip the excess butt.

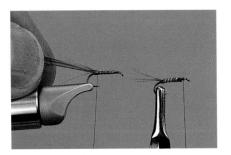

Alternate Step 3. An alternate body can be tied from turkey biots, the short, knife-blade fibers on the leading edge of a turkey wing flight feather. These feathers are available in all useful dyed colors. The biots make excellent segmented bodies. Clip several biots from the feather, and soak them in a damp paper towel until you're ready to use them. Tie in the biot by the tip on the near side of the hook, with the concave side toward you *(left)*, so that the trailing edge, when the biot is wound, will produce a ridgelike and segmented effect *(right)*. Use hackle pliers to wind the biot.

Step 4. Select two hen hackle feathers about as wide as one hook gap. Hold the feathers with their tips together, and measure them the length of the entire hook. Move the tie-in point just in front of the body, on top of the hook, with the feather stems toward the eye, the tips over the tails. Tie in the wings with a soft loop and several turns of thread forward. Take two to four figure eights of thread between the stems to hold the wings straight out to each side. Clip the excess stems.

Step 5. Select a hackle feather with fibers just short of the wing length. Tie it in behind the wings. Take two to four turns of hackle behind the wings and two to four turns in front. Tie it off and clip the excess tip. Form a neat thread head, whip-finish, clip the thread, and apply head cement. Clip hackle from the top and bottom, leaving only those fibers that stick out to the sides. For a simplified spentwing spinner, omit the wings and use only the hackle, trimmed top and bottom, to represent the wing venation of the natural insect.

Useful Variations

The Red Quill Spinner and Pale Morning Biot Spinner will cover most trout-stream spinner falls that you find in fishable numbers. The addition of the Blue Quill Spinner, which fishes for spinner falls of many little olives *(Baetis)* and lake speckle-wing quills *(Callibaetis),* and other colors as you need them, will enable you to cover specific spinner falls.

It's helpful to learn to tie spinner dressings both with hackle stem and with turkey biot bodies. Both materials are realistic in representing the segmentation of the slender naturals. Hackle stem is traditional and might look best. Stripped stems are now available dyed in many colors, or you can strip your own with bleach and dye them. Turkey biots come with so many to a single feather that the price becomes much lower than for dyed stem. On any of the listed dressings, you can use either stem or biot for the body.

| 1 | 2 | 3 |
| 4 | 5 | 6 |

1	Blue Quill Spinner
Hook	Standard dry fly, sizes 14, **16, 18**, 20
Thread	Gray 6/0 or 8/0
Tails	Blue dun hackle fibers, split
Body	Gray dyed hackle stem
Wings	Blue dun hen hackle tips
Hackle	Blue dun, clipped top and bottom

2	Ginger Quill Spinner
Hook	Standard dry fly, sizes 12, **14, 16**, 18
Thread	Tan 6/0 or 8/0
Tails	Ginger hackle fibers, split
Body	Ginger dyed hackle stem
Wings	Ginger hen hackle tips
Hackle	Ginger, clipped top and bottom

3	Pale Morning Quill Spinner
Hook	Standard dry fly, sizes 14, **16, 18**, 20
Thread	Pale yellow 6/0 or 8/0
Tails	Ginger hackle fibers, split
Body	Pale yellow dyed hackle stem
Wings	Ginger hen hackle tips
Hackle	Ginger, clipped top and bottom

4	Olive Quill Spinner
Hook	Standard dry fly, sizes 14, 16, **18, 20**
Thread	Olive 6/0 or 8/0
Tails	Blue dun hackle fibers, split
Body	Olive dyed hackle stem
Wings	Blue dun hen hackle tips
Hackle	Blue dun, clipped top and bottom

5	Pale Morning Biot Spinner
Hook	Standard dry fly, sizes 14, **16, 18**, 20
Thread	Tan 6/0 or 8/0
Tails	Ginger hackle fibers, split
Body	Pale yellow dyed turkey biot
Wings	Ginger hen hackle tips
Hackle	Ginger, clipped top and bottom

6	Trico Polypro Spinner
Hook	Standard dry fly, sizes 18, **20, 22**, 24
Thread	Black 6/0 or 8/0
Tails	White hackle fibers, split
Abdomen	Olive or black fur or synthetic dubbing
Wings	Light gray Polypro yarn
Thorax	Brown or black fur or synthetic dubbing
Hackle	None

Fishing Notes

You'll rarely find good spinner fishing on anything but smooth water. Mayflies deposit their eggs most often on pools or flats or they'd have drowned and depleted their species many generations ago. When they do fall on riffles or choppy runs, spinners are taken by trout just as readily, but almost always beneath the surface. You can imitate them best in mildly rough water with sparse wet flies fished on the swing, rather than with spentwing dry flies fished in the surface.

To fish spentwing spinners on smooth water during spinner falls, use your lightest tackle and a 12- to 15-foot leader with a 3-foot tippet of 5X, 6X, or even 7X if you absolutely must. If you go that fine, brace yourself to break off some nice trout, especially on the hook set.

Mark the lie of an individual trout carefully, and get into position to make a cross-stream reach cast or downstream wiggle cast. Time the trout's rise rhythm so that your fly drifts to it at the precise time the fish is ready to rise again. You often

A female spent spinner on the water in the position most naturals are in when taken by trout, and that your spinner dressings should imitate.

must cast again and again before everything becomes perfect in the eyes of the trout. They will not often break their rhythm, nor move very far out of a feeding lane, to take spent mayfly spinners. Little nutrition is left in the naturals, and trout seem aware of that.

WULFFS

These high-floating hairwing dry flies were designed by the late, famous Lee Wulff, who used them for Atlantic salmon as well as for trout. They are among the best for what I call *searching fishing,* where the object is to fish suspected lies in riffles and runs, drawing to the surface trout that are not either visible or actively feeding.

A good searching dry fly should be visible and look buggy to trout. It should also ride high and be easy for the fisherman to see. Flies in the Wulff series have all of these characteristics. The Royal Wulff, with its bright white wings, is possibly the most popular of all searching dry flies, ranking alongside the Adams and complementing it perfectly.

Use the drab Adams when you fish fairly smooth water, over somewhat educated trout. Use the Royal Wulff whenever the water is a bit rough, your trout haven't seen many flies in their wild lives, or you need to fish long casts to reach the water you believe holds trout and you cannot see the darker Adams on the water at such distance.

Royal Wulff	
LEE WULFF	
Hook	Standard dry fly, sizes 10, **12, 14,** 16
Thread	Black 6/0 or 8/0
Wings	White calf tail or calf body hair, upright and divided
Tail	Moose body hair
Body	Peacock herl, red floss, peacock herl
Hackle	Dark brown

Step 1. Layer the front half of the hook with thread. Clip a substantial patch of calf tail from the tail stem, clean fuzz and short fibers from the butts, and stack the hair. Calf tail is unruly. On size 14 and smaller flies, substitute calf body hair, which is easier to align. Measure the hair the length of the hook, and tie it in one-third the length of the shank behind the eye with ten to fifteen tight wraps of thread. Hold the wing up and brace enough layers of thread against the front of it to stand it upright. Clip the wing butts on a slant.

Step 2. Divide the wing hair in half, and take two or three thread Xs between the halves. Hold the tip of the far wing and wrap the thread up and around the base of it and between the wings to the near side. Hold the near wing tip and wrap the thread up and around the base of it and back between the wings to the far side. Repeat five to ten times, wrapping full figure eights around the wing bases to gather the fibers tightly together. Layer thread over the wing butts to the bend of the hook. Place a drop of head cement between the wings.

Step 3. Clip fifteen to twenty moose body hairs from the hide. Align the tips and measure the hair the length of the hook. Tie in the tail at the bend, and wrap thread over the butts to meet the wing butts. Trim the excess there and use thread wraps to create a tapered underbody. Return the thread to the base of the tail. Clip or strip two or three peacock fibers from an eyed feather. Tie them in with three to four soft turns of thread at the base of the tail. Twist the herl fibers together with the thread to form a herl rope, so the teeth of a few feisty trout will not cut the fragile herl.

Step 4. Take two or three turns of herl forward from the base of the tail, to form the rear third of the body. Untwist the herl from the working thread and use several thread turns forward to secure the herl over the next third of the body. Do not clip the excess herl. Clip 2 to 3 inches of red floss from the spool. Tie it in at the end of the herl butt. Return the thread to the midpoint of the hook.

Step 5. Wind two or three turns of floss forward. Tie it off and clip the excess. Twist the herl with the thread and take two or three turns forward. Untwist the herl, tie off the stems, and clip the excess. Leave a tiny gap between the end of the herl and the base of the wings. Select two neck hackle feathers with fibers one and a half to two hook gaps long, or use one long saddle feather. Strip webby fibers from the base, and pair the feathers back-to-back. Tie them in with the stems between the wings, using two to four turns of thread behind the wings and several more in front. Clip the stems.

Step 6. Wind the far hackle first, with three to four turns behind the wings, four to five in front. Tie off and clip the excess tip. Wind the second hackle through the first, with three or four turns behind the wings, the rest in front. Because the body is thicker than the head, three to four turns behind the wings will distribute as many hackle fibers as four to five turns in front of them. Tie off and clip the second hackle tip. Holding any stray fibers back out of the way, make a neat thread head and whip-finish the fly. Clip the thread and cement the head.

Useful Variations

The Royal Wulff and its variations do not imitate specific insects but look enough like a lot of the things that trout eat to make them excellent searching dry flies. They have roughly the shape of a mayfly dun. Some can be approximate solutions during hatches—for example, the Gray Wulff during a gray drake hatch or the Olive Wulff during a green drake hatch. Most, however, are not imitative and are best used when you're fishing the water rather than casting to selective rising trout.

Any other Wulff dressing will usually draw trout when the Royal Wulff works. The Royal Wulff is so effective, however, because trout favor it and it's easy for you to see on the water. I grew up fishing small streams for wild cutthroat trout, and it remains my favorite kind of fishing to this day. I developed the habit of trying the Royal Wulff first and switching to the drab-winged Grizzly Wulff if trout refuse the brighter fly. It's a strategy that has worked for me for thirty years.

When you pick searching dressings from any list of useful

variations, always start with a bright one and a drab one, such as a Royal Wulff and a Gray Wulff. Add others as you find situations that call for them.

| 1 | 2 | 3 |
| 4 | 5 | 6 |

1	Gray Wulff
Hook	Standard dry fly, sizes 10, **12, 14,** 16
Thread	Gray 6/0 or 8/0
Wings	Brown bucktail or deer body hair, upright and divided
Tail	Brown bucktail
Body	Muskrat fur dubbing
Hackle	Blue dun

2	Grizzly Wulff
Hook	Standard dry fly, sizes 10, **12, 14,** 16
Thread	Black 6/0 or 8/0
Wings	Brown bucktail or deer body hair, upright and divided
Tail	Brown bucktail
Body	Yellow floss
Hackle	Brown and grizzly

3	Olive Wulff
Hook	Standard dry fly, sizes 10, **12, 14,** 16
Thread	Olive 6/0 or 8/0
Wings	Gray dyed yearling elk body hair, upright and divided
Tail	Moose body hair
Body	Olive fur or synthetic dubbing
Hackle	Blue dun

4	Ausable Wulff
Hook	Standard dry fly, sizes 10, **12, 14,** 16
Thread	Red 6/0 or 8/0
Wings	White calf tail or calf body hair, upright and divided
Tail	Moose body hair
Body	Australian opossum fur dubbing
Hackle	Brown and grizzly

5	Blond Wulff
Hook	Standard dry fly, sizes 10, **12, 14,** 16
Thread	Black 6/0 or 8/0
Wings	Natural tan elk hair, upright and divided
Tail	Brown bucktail
Body	Cream fur or synthetic dubbing
Hackle	Ginger

6	House & Lot Variant
Hook	Standard dry fly, sizes 10, **12, 14,** 16
Thread	Black 6/0 or 8/0
Wings	White calf tail or calf body hair, upright and divided
Tail	White calf tail or calf body hair
Rib	Gold wire, reverse wrapped
Body	Rear half stripped peacock herl; front half peacock herl
Hackle	Badger

Fishing Notes

Large, bushy hairwing dry flies do not cast as easily as delicate drys tied for smoother water. It takes a 4- to 6-weight rod and line to boss them out and turn them over at the end of the cast. Your leader should be 9 to 12 feet long, tapered to 4X or 5X, depending on the size of the fly.

Thirty years ago, most Wulffs were tied in sizes 8 and 10, but I find that you get far more sure and solid strikes, fewer refusals, if you reduce their size to 12 or 14, even on big, rough rivers. On the smallest streams, I quickly switch to a size 16 Royal or Grizzly Wulff if trout move to a larger fly but refuse it at the last instant. If you get splashy rises but are frustrated because you can't get the hook set, go down in size and drabber in color, no matter what fly style you're using.

A favorite searching rig for riffles and runs, or even for smoother water where the trout are not pestered to death, is a size 12 or 14 Royal Wulff with a size 14 or 16 beadhead nymph tied directly to the hook bend on a 20-inch tippet. This combination offers trout a choice of both fly pattern and type

Wulff drys are perfect for small or rough waters, where trout are not selective and must make quick decisions.

of fly. It fools quite a few more fish than either fly does when fished alone. Whether you fish a Wulff dressing by itself or with a dropper, it's usually cast over the kind of water where an up-and-across-stream presentation is most effective.

HUMPIES

The Humpy style of dry fly is one of the buggiest, and it's one of the best for searching the water when no hatch is happening. The fat body of the fly, with its deer-hair shellback, can give the impression of a portly mayfly, caddis, stonefly, grasshopper, or beetle on the water. Trout can mistake it for many things, which is why it works much of the time. In larger sizes, 10 and 12, it looks like a big enough bite up there to make the trip to the top worthwhile. It is surprisingly effective in smaller sizes, 14 and 16, as well.

The original Humpy, with its yellow underbody and natural deer-hair wing, is the most important dressing in the style because it resembles the most food forms: yellow-bodied mayfly duns and caddis adults, golden stoneflies, and hoppers. The second most important fly in the style is the Royal Humpy, with its white wing, which entices almost as many trout and is much easier for the angler to see afloat on the water. Try those first, and tie others if the style catches fish for you and you'd like to fish it in a wider array of colors.

Humpy	
Hook	Standard dry fly, sizes 10, **12, 14,** 16
Thread	Yellow 6/0 or 8/0
Tail	Natural deer body hair
Wing	Natural deer body hair, upright and divided
Underbody	Working thread over wing butts
Shellback	Wing hair drawn forward over body
Hackle	Grizzly and brown

Step 1. Secure the hook in the vise, and layer the shank with thread. Clean fuzz and short hairs from the butts of a small patch of deer hair, and align the tips in your stacker. Tie in the tail, and hold the tail butts against the shank with your off hand while running thread wraps forward over them to the midpoint of the shank. Take a tight layer of thread back to the tail base and forward to the midpoint. Make the farthest turns back on the tail soft to keep from flaring the hollow hair excessively. Trim the excess butts, and cover them with tight thread wraps.

Step 2. Clip a substantial patch of deer hair from the hide—more than you think you need. Clean the butts and align the tips. Measure the hair from the hook eye to the end of the tail, or two full hook lengths. Hold the hair in a tight pinch in your off-hand thumb and forefinger, and clip the excess butts straight across *before* tying the hair in. Move the pinch to the midpoint of the hook and tie in the wing tightly there. Hold the hair to the hook shank, and run thread wraps back and forth to cover it from the tie-in point to the base of the tail, forming the thread body.

Step 3. Separate the longer wing hair from the shorter tail hair. Gather the wing tips and draw the wing forward, twisting it slightly. Tie it off at the end of the body. Stand the wing upright with layers of thread jammed tight against the front. The wing should be the length of the hook. If you measured the hair too short in Step 2, you will not be able to separate the wing from the tail, and the wing will be stubby. If you measured the hair too long, the wing will stand too tall in Step 3. This fly requires practice; tie by the dozen.

Step 4. Separate the wing material into equal halves with your fingers. Take two or three thread **X**s between the wings to hold them apart. Take five figure eights, each down and around the far wing, back up and over between the wings, then down and around the near wing, just as you did to secure the wing bases on the Royal Wulff. As an alternative, you can wind the thread around each wing base five times. Place a drop of head cement between the wings to soak into the thread wraps.

Step 5. Select a grizzly and a brown hackle feather with fibers one and a half to two hook gaps, just shorter than the upright wings. Remove webby fibers from the base of each feather. Pair them with their concave sides together, and tie them on top of the hook shank with the stems between the wings. The concave sides of the feathers should face you, so that the hackle when wound will have a slight forward tilt. Use two turns of thread behind the wings, five or six in front. Clip the excess stems behind the hook eye.

Step 6. Wind the first hackle, taking two or three turns behind the wings, the rest in front. Tie it off and clip the excess tip. Wind the second hackle through the first, again with two or three turns behind the wings, the rest in front. Tie it off and clip the excess tip. Leave plenty of room in front of the wings for the head. It is easy to crowd it and not have room to properly finish the fly. Hold any stray hackle fibers back out of the way with a triangle made with the tips of the forefinger, middle finger, and thumb of your off hand. Use a few thread wraps to make a neat head. Whip-finish the fly, clip the thread, and cement the head.

Useful Variations

Beyond the original Humpy and its drab Adams and Olive variations, the style becomes fancy; the colors are not those of nature but those that have caught the imagination of a tier. Useful most often in searching situations, not during hatches, the Royal, Blond, Orange, and Black Humpies catch fish in surprising numbers. I recommend that you tie and carry the Royal Humpy as a backup to the original Humpy for your basic dry-fly box. Use the yellow-bodied original for searching fishing, so long as you're able to see it on the water, or when grasshoppers, caddis, or golden stoneflies are out and you have no accurate imitation. Use the Royal Humpy when you want to fish a buggy fly with a bright wing that's easy to see. Tie and try the others as you desire.

The wing hair on the Royal Humpy does not form the shellback, as it does on all other Humpies. Tie in the wings first, following the directions in Steps 1 and 2 for the Royal Wulff. Tie in the tail, then cut, stack, and tie in a separate section of moose body hair for the shellback. Layer thread over the butts for the underbody, then draw the hair forward, twist it slightly, and tie it off behind the wings. Clip the excess tips, leaving a slight gap for the hackle.

1	2	3
4	5	6

1	Royal Humpy
Hook	Standard dry fly, sizes 10, **12, 14,** 16
Thread	Red 6/0 or 8/0
Wings	White calf tail or calf body hair
Tail	Moose body hair
Underbody	Working thread over shellback butts
Shellback	Moose body hair
Hackle	Brown

2	Adams Humpy
Hook	Standard dry fly, sizes 10, **12, 14,** 16
Thread	Gray 6/0 or 8/0
Tail	Moose body hair
Wing	Gray yearling elk or deer body hair
Underbody	Working thread over wing butts
Overbody	Wing hair drawn forward
Hackle	Grizzly and brown

3	Blond Humpy
Hook	Standard dry fly, sizes 10, **12, 14,** 16
Thread	Yellow 6/0 or 8/0
Tail	Brown bucktail
Wing	Bleached yearling elk hair
Underbody	Working thread over wing butts
Overbody	Wing hair drawn forward
Hackle	Ginger

4	Olive Humpy
Hook	Standard dry fly, sizes 10, **12, 14,** 16
Thread	Olive 6/0 or 8/0
Tail	Moose body hair
Wing	Gray yearling elk or deer hair
Underbody	Working thread over wing butts
Overbody	Wing hair drawn forward
Hackle	Brown

5	Orange Humpy
Hook	Standard dry fly, sizes 10, **12, 14,** 16
Thread	Orange 6/0 or 8/0
Tail	Moose body hair
Wing	Moose body hair
Underbody	Working thread over wing butts
Overbody	Wing hair drawn forward
Hackle	Brown

6	Black Humpy
Hook	Standard dry fly, sizes 10, **12, 14,** 16
Thread	Black 6/0 or 8/0
Tail	Moose body hair
Wing	Moose body hair
Underbody	Working thread over wing butts
Overbody	Wing hair drawn forward
Hackle	Dark blue dun or black

Fishing Notes

Humpies are bulky for their size and are designed to be fished over somewhat rough water. Use a 4- to 6-weight outfit, which should be your standard dry-fly rod anyway. Stouten the leader a bit: 3X for size 10 flies, 4X for sizes 12 and 14, and 5X for size 16 or smaller. Always dress Humpies well with dry-fly floatant before fishing them. Whenever the fly begins to sink, bring it in, squeeze water out of the portly body, and redress it.

Cast over any suspected holding lies: in front of and behind boulders, along the shoreline wherever the current works along it, and the length of any seam where two currents meet. It is difficult to tell where trout might hold in a uniform riffle or un-featured run. Make disciplined casts to drift your Humpy in parallel lines a foot apart to cover all of the water.

The upstream cast works best on most water where you'll fish Humpies. If you do use them on smooth water over rising trout, the best position and presentation allow you to get a drag-free drift over trout without alarming them with the line and leader.

Humpies are excellent for covering the water in broad riffles on big rivers such as the Deschutes.

PARACHUTE DRY FLIES

Parachute drys are unusual in that they float very well while at the same time lowering the body into the surface film, showing trout a silhouette similar to that of an insect at rest on the water. They can be at once excellent searching dry flies and great imitations. Flies in this style can be cast to riffles and runs to drum up willing fish or fished on smooth water over selective trout. If your waters are freestone and somewhat rough but also a bit heavily fished, parachute drys offer you a way to show the trout something different from the normal run of hackled dressings that they see daily and learn to refuse. Yet you won't sacrifice any flotation.

The Parachute Adams, with its visible white wing, natural gray body color, and smoke of mixed hackle, looks like a lot of things in nature that trout make a living eating. It is one of the best searching dry flies you can carry and is a critical fly for your minimal list of patterns. Tie it in sizes 14, 16, and 18. It will catch trout on smooth and rough waters, when they are selective and when they are not.

Parachute Adams

Hook	Standard dry fly, sizes 12, **14**, **16**, **18**
Thread	Black 6/0 or 8/0
Wingpost	White calf body hair
Tail	Grizzly and brown hackle fibers
Body	Muskrat fur dubbing
Hackle	Grizzly and brown, one size oversize

Step 1. Layer thread over the front half of the hook. Clip a patch of calf body hair, clean fuzz from the butts, and align the tips in your stacker. Measure the hair just the length of the hook shank; if the wing is too tall, the fly will tip over when fished. Tie in the wing one-third the shank length behind the eye, and clip the butts on a bias. Stand the wing up with a thread dam. Gather the wing-tip fibers in your off hand, and take eight to ten thread turns around the base. Wrap thread over the wing butts to the bend of the hook.

Step 2. Peel or clip six to ten long, web-free grizzly hackle fibers, and an equal amount of brown fibers, from rooster neck side feathers—called *spades*—and align the tips. You can hold the first color in your hackle pliers while you clip the second, then meld them. Measure the tail the length of the hook, including the eye and bend. Tie in the tail at the bend of the hook. Wrap thread over the tail butts to the wing butts before clipping the excess. This forms a tapered underbody for the fur dubbing.

Step 3. Cut a small amount of muskrat fur from the hide. The underbody is already built up, and you need only enough fur to cover it. Remove guard hairs from the fur, and twist the fur onto the thread in a thin skein just long enough to reach the base of the wing. Wind the body to that point and stop. The result should be a slender, tapered body. Your model here is the delicate body of a natural mayfly dun.

Step 4. Select a grizzly and a brown hackle feather with fibers the length of the entire hook shank, one size oversize to keep the fly from tipping over when fished. Use short feathers from the sides of the necks. You need only four turns from each, and it's a shame to waste most of a better feather that would give you ten turns. Strip fuzz from the bases of the feathers, pair them with their concave sides facing down, and tie them in on the far side of the shank, in front of the wing. Clip the excess stems.

Step 5. Twist a short skein of muskrat fur onto the thread. Take one turn behind the wingpost and over the hackle stems, then taper dubbing to the hook eye. Grasp the top hackle in your hackle pliers. Wind one turn around the wingpost *counterclockwise*. You might need to hold the wingpost tip while making this first wrap. Tuck three more turns, each beneath the one before it, down to the body of the fly. Drape the hackle pliers over the shank just behind the hook eye, and tug the hackle tip tight. Tie the hackle off with three to four turns of thread.

Step 6. Clip the first hackle tip. Wind the second hackle four turns counterclockwise around the wingpost, each tucked under the one before it. Drape the hackle pliers over the shank, tug the hackle tip tight, tie it off, and clip the excess tip. Use a triangle formed with the tips of your off-hand forefinger, middle finger, and thumb to draw all hackle fibers up and back from the eye. Form a neat thread head, whip-finish, and clip the thread. Clip any stray hackle fibers. Cement the head; place a generous drop of head cement to soak into the wingpost base.

Useful Variations

The secrets to a useful parachute tie are the short wingpost and oversize hackle, both of which keep the fly from lying on its side when it lands on the water. Winding the hackle counterclockwise, so that your thread wraps, when you tie each hackle off, go in the same direction and secure it rather than opposing it and therefore loosening it, combines with the drop of head cement at the base of the wingpost to keep the fly from unraveling on the first or tenth trout.

Almost any dry-fly style can be tied as a parachute variation. Most will be effective, though not necessarily any more effective than the original tie. Many flies, however, work best for certain purposes when tied as parachutes. For example, A. K. Best's Olive Quill Parachute and PMD Quill Parachute, from his book *A. K.'s Fly Box* (Lyons & Burford, 1996), lower their hackle stem bodies to the water when tied in parachute style. They fish better over smooth-water hatches than versions tied with the hackle wound as a traditional collar.

Some of the following dressings are searching flies. Others are imitative. Still others bridge that gap. I use Skip Morris's

Olive Parachute, for example, on rough water or on lightly fished streams whenever mayflies are hatching and trout demand the mayfly shape but are not fussy about a precise match in terms of color. When using one hackle rather than two, as in the Olive Parachute, wind just five to six turns.

1	2	3
4	5	6

1	Olive Parachute		2	Hare's Ear Parachute		3	Float-N-Fool
	SKIP MORRIS			ED SCHROEDER			WAYNE BUSZEK
Hook	Standard dry fly, sizes **12, 14,** 16, 18		Hook	Standard dry fly, sizes **12, 14,** 16, 18		Hook	Standard dry fly, sizes **12, 14,** 16, 18
Thread	Olive 6/0 or 8/0		Thread	Tan 6/0 or 8/0		Thread	Black 6/0 or 8/0
Wingpost	Yellow Polypro yarn		Wingpost	White calf body hair		Wingpost	Butts of tail hair
Tail	Black moose body hair		Tail	Brown bucktail		Tail	White calf body hair
Body	Olive fur or synthetic dubbing		Body	Hare's mask fur		Rib	Fine gold wire, reverse wrapped
Hackle	Dark blue dun, one size oversize		Hackle	Grizzly, one size oversize		Body	Peacock herl
						Hackle	Brown and grizzly, one size oversize

4	Olive Quill Parachute		5	PMD Quill Parachute		5	Parachute Caddis
	A. K. BEST			A. K. BEST			ED SCHROEDER
Hook	Standard dry fly, size 14, 16, **18, 20**		Hook	Standard dry fly, sizes 14, **16, 18,** 20		Hook	Standard dry fly, sizes **12, 14,** 16, 18
Thread	Olive 6/0 or 8/0		Thread	Pale yellow 6/0 or 8/0		Thread	Cream 6/0 or 8/0
Wingpost	White turkey flats		Wingpost	White turkey flat		Wingpost	White calf body hair
Tail	Blue dun hackle fibers, slightly splayed, using a slight thread lump		Tail	Ginger hackle fibers, slightly splayed		Body	Hare's mask fur
Body	Olive dyed hackle stem		Body	Yellow-olive dyed hackle stem		Wing	Mottled turkey feather section
Hackle	Blue dun, one size oversize		Hackle	Ginger, one size oversize		Hackle	Grizzly, one size oversize

Fishing Notes

Parachutes are useful as searching dressings over rough water, but can also be used as imitations when trout are sipping selectively to insects on very smooth water. The Parachute Adams is used in both of these ways.

On rough water, your leader should be about the length of your rod, with a 2-foot tippet of 4X or 5X, depending on the fly size. You'll usually be wading upstream, casting to prospective holding lies, covering all of the water. The up-and-across-stream presentation suits this sort of fishing perfectly.

If you're casting parachutes as imitative dressings to rising trout on smooth water, use your most delicate rod and lightest line. Lengthen your leader to 12 to 15 feet, with a fine 3- to 4-foot tippet. The cross-stream reach cast and downstream wiggle cast will serve you best for this kind of demanding fishing.

Parachute drys are excellent for fishing hatches and also for exploring water with flats and riffles.

ELK HAIR CADDIS

Al Troth, the famous Dillon, Montana, tier and guide, created the Elk Hair Caddis to capture the shape of the natural caddis adult and to float well on his rough western rivers. Caddisflies are almost always out dancing over trout streams. Trout are usually happy to take one, or a fly that looks like one. As a searching dry fly, the Elk Hair Caddis is on even terms with the Adams and Royal Wulff.

If you fish in the West, the Elk Hair Caddis in a range of sizes should occupy a few prime compartments in your dry-fly box. It will catch fish for you in the East as well, and anywhere else in the world you might find trout. So will the many variations that have been created upon it.

The original tan tie is used most because it's easiest to see. I list it with a warning: I tied it for many years with materials that became brighter and brighter so I could see it better and better. Trout began to refuse it. I toned it back down to the original materials—natural elk hair rather than bleached, medium ginger hackle rather than light—and trout began taking the fly eagerly once again. It can be far from drab, but not brashly bright. On size 16 and smaller Elk Hair Caddis and its variations, the hackle and wire rib are often omitted if the fly is to be fished on smooth water.

Elk Hair Caddis

AL TROTH

Hook	Standard dry fly, sizes **12**, **14**, 16, 18
Thread	Tan 6/0 or 8/0
Rib	Fine gold wire, counterwound over hackle
Body	Tan fur or synthetic dubbing
Hackle	Ginger, palmered over body
Wing	Natural tan elk or yearling elk

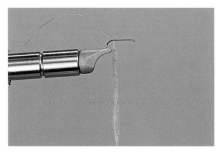

Step 1. Debarb the hook, insert it in the vise, and start the thread just behind the eye. Clip 2 to 4 inches of ribbing wire from the spool. Hold it along the hook shank, capture it with the thread, and take thread wraps over it to the bend of the hook. Place it out of the way in the materials clip if your vise has one. Select a fine dubbing fur or synthetic that is tan but not bright. Twist the dubbing to the thread without taper, somewhat thicker than you use on most dry flies; the body of a natural caddis is a bit portly.

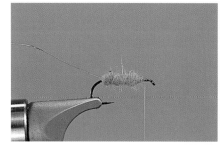

Step 2. Wind the body forward to a point about one-fifth the shank length behind the hook eye. The body of a caddis imitation should be fat compared with the body of mayfly dressings and should have no taper at all or even a reverse taper. Natural caddis bodies are sometimes bulbous at the back end.

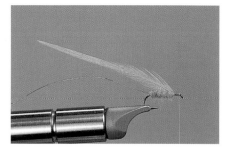

Step 3. Select a hackle feather with fibers no more than one and a half times the hook gap. Undersize is better than oversize in this style, to keep the finished fly from rolling on its side when fished. You need ten to twelve turns of hackle. Use a grade 1 or grade 2 neck feather. Saddle hackle also works well. Strip webby fibers from the lower stem, and tie in the feather at the end of the body.

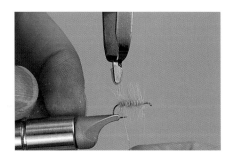

Step 4. Wind the hackle to the hook bend in evenly spaced turns. Hold the hackle pliers above the bend of the hook with your off hand, and counterwind one full turn of ribbing wire over the hackle stem with your tying hand. This first turn of wire secures the hackle tip. Twitch the hackle pliers forward briskly to break the stem against the wire. Take four to six turns of ribbing wire forward to the hook eye. Wobble the wire back and forth as you go to avoid matting down excess hackle fibers. Tie off the wire and either clip or break off the excess.

Step 5. Clip a fair clump of elk hair from the hide. Only experience, tying by the half dozen or more, will tell you the precise amount for each size of fly you tie. Yearling elk, or calf, is the best material for this style of fly. If you buy patches in natural, bleached, dyed brown, and dyed gray, you'll have most of the hair you need for this and a few other styles of dry flies, such as the Hairwing Duns. Clean fuzz from the butts of the hair, align the tips in your stacker, and measure the hair the length of the entire hook.

Step 6. Hold the wing hair in a tight pinch just behind the hook eye, and draw a soft loop tightly down over it. Continuing to hold the wing in your pinch, take ten to fifteen wraps of thread back over the hair. The wing and butts should stand at 45-degree angles to the shank, with a noticeable gap between them. Draw the hair butts back and up with your off hand, and tuck several thread turns between the eye and the butts to prop them up. Whip-finish the head once or twice, and clip the thread. Gather the butts in your off hand and clip them just in front of the hook eye.

Useful Variations

Endless variations have been worked on the Elk Hair Caddis. The original is the most useful as a searching dry fly because it is the most visible on the water. If trout refuse it, try one of the darker variations listed below.

Jim Schollmeyer's Deer Hair Caddis is the variation I use most. It resembles the prolific gray sedges, which are among the most abundant trout-stream insects all over the world. This fly can be used when the insects are out or when they're not; the Deer Hair Caddis always seems to remind trout of something they've eaten lately. I tie a variation of the style with a brown wing, peacock herl body, and grizzly hackle. It resembles spotted sedges, which often outnumber gray sedges, especially in tailwaters. My own Beetle Bug Caddis, with its red body and gray wing, seems to arouse drowsy trout. I use it most often on small streams.

Craig Mathews's X-Caddis is an emerger style based on the Elk Hair that extends its usefulness to smooth water. The absence of hackle allows the body to rest in the surface film. The

tail represents the cast pupal shuck of the natural. Fish the X-Caddis over selective trout feeding on hatching caddis.

1	2	3
4	5	6

1	Deer Hair Caddis		2	Brown Elk Hair Caddis		3	Gray Deer Hair Caddis
	JIM SCHOLLMEYER		Hook	Standard dry fly, sizes **12, 14,** 16, 18		Hook	Standard dry fly, sizes 12, **14, 16,** 18
Hook	Standard dry fly, sizes **12, 14,** 16, 18		Thread	Brown 6/0 or 8/0		Thread	Gray 6/0 or 8/0
Thread	Olive 6/0 or 8/0		Rib	Gold wire or working thread, counterwound over hackle		Rib	Gold wire or working thread, counterwound over hackle
Rib	Gold wire or working thread, counterwound over hackle		Body	Peacock herl		Body	Muskrat fur or gray synthetic dubbing
Body	Olive fur or synthetic dubbing		Hackle	Grizzly, palmered over body		Hackle	Blue dun, palmered over body
Hackle	Blue dun, palmered over body, V-notch clipped out of bottom		Wing	Brown deer or yearling elk hair		Wing	Gray deer or yearling elk hair
Wing	Gray deer or yearling elk hair						

4	Beetle Bug Caddis		5	Olive X-Caddis		6	Tan X-Caddis
	DAVE HUGHES			CRAIG MATHEWS			CRAIG MATHEWS
Hook	Standard dry fly, sizes **12, 14,** 16, 18		Hook	Standard dry fly, sizes 12, 14, **16, 18**		Hook	Standard dry fly, sizes 12, **14, 16,** 18
Thread	Gray 6/0 or 8/0		Thread	Olive 6/0 or 8/0		Thread	Tan 6/0 or 8/0
Rib	Gold wire or working thread, counterwound over hackle		Trailing shuck	Amber Z-lon		Trailing shuck	Amber Z-lon
Body	Red fur or synthetic dubbing		Body	Olive fur or synthetic dubbing		Body	Tan fur or synthetic dubbing
Hackle	Brown, palmered over body		Wing	Gray deer or yearling elk hair		Wing	Tan deer or yearling elk hair
Wing	Light gray dyed deer or yearling elk hair						

Fishing Notes

The Elk Hair Caddis style is designed to be fished on brisk water. The flies float well, ride high, and are visible to both fish and fisherman. Like most good searching flies, they are based closely on an abundant trout food form.

Use Elk Hair Caddis drys with your standard trout-fly gear in the 4- to 6-weight class with tippets stout enough to turn over such heavily hackled flies. It's fine to take your position downstream from the trout, or their prospective lies, in such rough water and to fish with the standard upstream presentation.

The original Elk Hair Caddis, or one of its hackled variations, is the perfect platform to support a beadhead nymph one size smaller. Tie the nymph to a 20-inch tippet, one size finer than the tippet to the dry fly, right to the bend of the dry. Fish them both with careful casts and open loops to keep them from tangling in the air. Set the hook if the dry fly disappears—that's a trout taking the nymph.

A perfect riffle corner to search with a high-floating Elk Hair Caddis style of dry fly.

QUILL-WING CADDIS

The natural caddis adult has a tent-shaped wing held low over a fairly fat body. Flies that work best on trout feeding selectively to caddis, especially on smooth water where they can get a good look at the natural or its imitation, show an unobstructed silhouette of the caddis body and wing on the water. The Quill-Wing Caddis style does this best. It is an excellent complement to the Elk Hair Caddis style, which fishes best on rougher water. Carry representative sizes and colors of the two styles in your basic set of flies, and you'll be able to match caddis on any water type where trout take them.

Quill-Wing Caddis are simple to tie. Spray the feathers ahead of time with artist's fixative and give it time to dry. If you use a feather without fixative, it will tatter either in the tying or on the first few casts.

The late Wayne Buszek's Kings River Caddis was one of the first and is still one of the best quill-wing caddis dressings. It captures the colors of many natural caddis. Nature offers far too many caddis species to imitate each one, as we often do with mayflies. With caddis, it's often best to settle on dressings that average quite a few of them out.

Kings River Caddis

WAYNE BUSZEK

Hook	Standard dry fly, sizes 12, **14, 16,** 18
Thread	Brown 6/0 or 8/0
Body	Tannish brown fur or synthetic dubbing
Wing	Mottled turkey feather section
Hackle	Brown

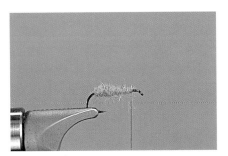

Step 1. Debarb the hook, insert it in the vise, and layer the shank with thread. Twist dubbing to the thread, making it a bit fatter near the hook and thinner as you move away from it. The resulting body will be thicker in the back and middle sections, tapered down toward the front. Wind the body forward, ending about one-fourth the hook-shank length behind the eye. The slender front helps when you fold the turkey feather section for the wing around the body.

Step 2. Prepare a mottled turkey tail feather by spraying it with artist's fixative and letting it dry. If you buy a matched pair and spray both, you'll find many other uses for them, such as wings on Muddler Minnows. Cut a section of feather a bit wider than the hook gap. Fold the section gently, and clip it on a bias at the thicker end. Tying it in by the thinner, softer end makes it easier to fold without the section separating, which it's going to do the first time a fish whacks it, anyway.

Step 3. Measure the wing just past the end of the hook bend, and fold it around the front end of the body. Tie it in with a soft loop and secure it with several more turns of thread forward almost to the hook eye. Clip the excess wing butts behind the eye. The biggest problem can arise here: If the body is too long and you tie in the wing at the end of it, you won't have enough room left for the hackle and head. Be sure when tying in the body and wing that you leave room to finish the fly.

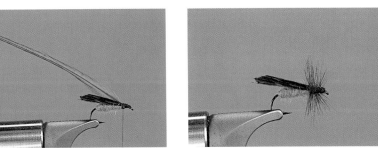

Step 4. Select a high-quality hackle with fibers just one and a half times the hook gap. Don't use oversize hackle or the fly will stand too high off the water. You need eight to ten turns of hackle. If your hackle is not high quality, you can use two feathers or a single saddle feather. Prepare the hackle by stripping webby fibers from the base. Tie it in with the concave side toward you so that when wound, the fibers stand straight up or lean forward, not back.

Step 5. Wind the hackle, spreading it over the front quarter of the hook shank, from the base of the wing to just behind the hook eye. Be sure to leave room in this step for the head and whip finish. Tie off the hackle, clip the excess tip, form a neat thread head, and whip-finish the fly. Cement the head and clear the hook eye. The fly is now finished, and this is the way it is fished most often.

Step 6. If you desire to present this fly flush in the surface film, for fishing over water that is somewhat smooth and trout that are quite selective, clip a **V**-notch out of the hackle on the bottom. This lowers the body, but it impairs flotation, so don't do this for flies you plan to fish on riffles and runs. I prefer to place all of my Quill-Wing Caddis dressings into the fly box with full hackle and trim them later, out on the stream or lake, if the situation calls for it.

Useful Variations

The Kings River Caddis fishes well for the spotted sedges, a caddis group of about forty-five species. These naturals have brown wings and tan to brown bodies. Their larvae spin nets to capture particles of drift. Plankton is delivered in abundance below dams; tailwaters are prime water for spotted sedges, selective trout, and the Kings River Caddis.

Brown and Gray Quill-Wing Caddis variations are effective when naturals in those colors emerge on smooth water. Gray sedges are second in abundance to spotted sedges but arise from larvae that live in riffles and runs. The Gray Quill-Wing Caddis works well at the edges of fast water. The Deer Hair Caddis is a better choice for gray sedges in the fast water where the naturals are most abundant.

The Henryville Special and Hemingway Caddis are two Quill-Wing Caddis ties that fish well both East and West. They are excellent searching dressings whenever a few caddis adults are present, trout are sipping them, and the water is smooth enough that you'd rather fish a more imitative style than the Elk Hair Caddis or one of its heavily hackled variations.

The Tentwing Caddis and Flatwing Caddis have the hackles trimmed to lower the body of the fly flush with the surface film. They fish best on flat water.

1	2	3
4	5	6

1	Brown Quill-Wing Caddis
Hook	Standard dry fly, sizes **12**, **14**, 16, 18
Thread	Brown 6/0 or 8/0
Body	Brown fur or synthetic dubbing
Wing	Mottled turkey feather section
Hackle	Brown

2	Gray Quill-Wing Caddis
Hook	Standard dry fly, sizes 12, **14**, **16**, 18
Thread	Olive 6/0 or 8/0
Body	Dark olive fur or synthetic dubbing
Wing	Dark mallard or goose wing feather section
Hackle	Dark blue dun

3	Henryville Special
	HIRAM BROBST
Hook	Standard dry fly, sizes 12, **14**, **16**, 18
Thread	Black 6/0 or 8/0
Rib	Undersize grizzly hackle
Body	Olive fur or synthetic dubbing
Underwing	Wood duck flank fibers
Wing	Mallard wing feather section
Hackle	Dark ginger

4	Hemingway Caddis
	RENÉ HARROP AND JACK HEMINGWAY
Hook	Standard dry fly, sizes 12, **14**, **16**, 18
Thread	Olive 6/0 or 8/0
Rib	Undersize blue dun hackle
Body	Olive fur or synthetic dubbing
Underwing	Wood duck flank fibers
Wing	Mallard wing feather section
Thorax	Peacock herl
Hackle	Blue dun, wound over thorax

5	Tentwing Caddis
Hook	Standard dry fly, sizes 12, **14**, **16**, 18
Thread	Black 6/0 or 8/0
Body	Pheasant tail fibers wound as herl
Hackle	Dark ginger, clipped top and bottom
Wing	Mottled turkey feather section

6	Flatwing Caddis
Hook	Standard dry fly, sizes 12, **14**, **16**, 18
Thread	Gray 6/0 or 8/0
Rib	Undersize brown hackle, trimmed top and bottom
Body	Muskrat fur or gray synthetic dubbing
Wing	Mottled turkey feather section
Hackle	Brown, trimmed top and bottom

Fishing Notes

The Quill-Wing Caddis series is designed to match caddis hatches on smooth water. The best time to fish them is when a particular caddis is abundant and trout are concentrating on them. This is usually on pools and flats, not riffles and runs. You will use these flies more often on spring creeks and tailwaters than on freestone streams. Let your fishing predict your tying: Add a few of these to your basic selection if you fish often on silky currents. Begin with the Kings River Caddis in sizes 14 and 16. Add the Henryville Special in sizes 16 and 18. Follow with others if you find that trout request them.

In the sorts of situations where you'll fish these imitative caddis dressings, it's best to rig up with your most delicate gear and use long leaders with fine tippets. Wade into position as close as you can to the trout without alerting them to your presence. The cross-stream reach cast and downstream wiggle cast are more effective than the traditional upstream dry-fly cast.

Wherever caddis hatches are important on somewhat smooth water, quill-wing drys show an excellent silhouette, much like the natural, to trout.

STONEFLY DRYS

The two largest stonefly species, the salmon fly and golden stone, are the most important hatches in the order. Both are predominantly western. Many other groups, including little brown stones, yellow sallies, and olive sallies, are important in the East, the West, and everywhere in between. All stoneflies live only in moving water.

It's important to fish the correct imitation whenever a stonefly species is on the water in good numbers. Trout key on them and refuse everything else. It's also important to know that some stonefly dressings, such as Randall Kaufmann's Stimulator, when tied in smaller sizes will also take trout during caddis and grasshopper activity. They make excellent searching dressings.

The listed Improved Sofa Pillow is the standard dressing for the riotous salmon fly hatch on the Deschutes in Oregon, the Snake in Idaho, and the Madison, the Big Hole, and the Yellowstone in Montana. The Golden Improved Sofa Pillow and the Yellow Stimulator are standard for golden stones.

Improved Sofa Pillow	
Hook	3X or 4X long, sizes 4, **6**, **8**, 10, 12
Thread	Black 6/0
Tail	Natural yearling elk
Rib	Fine gold wire counterwound over body hackle
Body hackle	Brown, undersize
Body	Burnt or rusty orange fur or synthetic dubbing
Wing	Natural yearling elk
Hackle	Brown

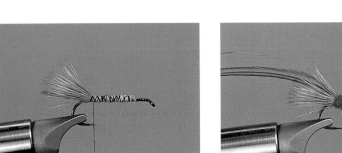

Step 1. Debarb the hook, fix it in the vise, and layer the shank with thread. Select a patch of elk hair about the size of a wing for an Elk Hair Caddis. The hair should be bright enough that it's easy for you to see but not bleached, so that it's not so bright that trout will turn away from it. Clean fuzz from the hair butts, align the tips in your stacker, and measure the hair half the length of the hook shank. Tie it in at the bend of the hook, and wrap the butts forward two-thirds of the shank length before trimming the excess.

Step 2. Tie in 3 to 4 inches of gold ribbing wire at the base of the tail. This is used to protect the ribbing hackle from the teeth of trout. Select a long hackle, either neck or saddle, with fibers just one hook gap long. Strip webby fibers from the lower stem, and tie in the hackle at the base of the tail, with the concave side toward you so the fibers lean a bit forward when wound. Twist dubbing onto the thread, and wind a stout, untapered body over the rear two-thirds of the hook shank.

Step 3. Wind the body hackle forward in evenly spaced wraps to the end of the body. Tie it off and clip or break off the excess tip. You should be working a full third of the shank length behind the hook eye at this point. Leave plenty of room for the wing and final hackle. Counterwind the ribbing wire through the body hackle. Wobble the wire back and forth as you wind it to prevent knocking down too many hackle fibers, though you'll always catch a few.

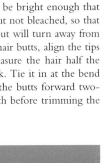

Step 4. Select a patch of elk hair about twice the thickness of the tail. Clip it from the hide, clean fuzz from the butts, and align the tips in your stacker. Hold the wing in a firm pinch in your tying hand, and measure it to the end of the tail. When tied, you want the end of the wing to stand either even with or just short of the end of the tail. The tail, when the fly is on the water, represents the back end of the wing, not the actual tails of the insect, which are insignificant to an imitation.

Step 5. Transfer the wing pinch to your off hand, and hold the wing tie-in point firmly in place at the end of the body. Tie in the wing, winding several thread wraps forward over the flared hair butts. Gather the butts and clip them on a long slant. Cover them with thread forward to a point just behind the hook eye. This should cover the front quarter of the hook shank. Use thread wraps to make an even taper over the butts, rather than a sharp shoulder, so you can wind the hackle down it without slippage.

Step 6. Select a single saddle or two neck hackles with fibers one and a half to two hook gaps long. Strip webby fibers from the base of the stem. If you're using one saddle, tie it in with the concave side toward you so the fibers tilt forward when wound. If you use two neck hackles, pair them back-to-back so the fibers are well spread when wound. Finish the fly by winding the hackle over the front quarter of the hook shank. Tie off, clip the excess, form a neat thread head, and whip-finish.

Useful Variations

The stonefly order comes in a fairly distinct set of colors and sizes: the giant salmon fly, with its almost black body that's salmon-orange on the underside; the slightly smaller golden stone; the small yellow sallies; and two tiny groups, the little brown stones and the olive sallies. If you tie listed variations of the Improved Sofa Pillow to cover these, you'll be prepared for any stonefly event.

Those stonefly drys most likely to be useful to you during hatches are the standard Improved Sofa Pillow and the Golden Improved Sofa Pillow and, if you encounter smaller hatches, the Yellow and Olive Sallies. As a searching dressing, it's hard to beat the Yellow Stimulator. It looks like so many things trout eat that they're almost always glad to get one. Tie and carry it in sizes 8 through 12, and give it a prominent place in your basic dry-fly box, whether or not you fish stonefly hatches.

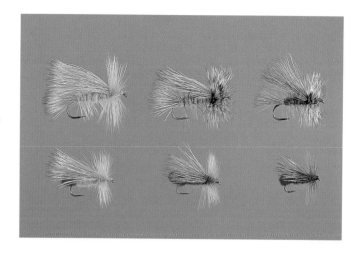

| 1 | 2 | 3 |
| 4 | 5 | 6 |

1	Golden Improved Sofa Pillow		2	Yellow Stimulator		3	Green Stimulator
				RANDALL KAUFMANN			RANDALL KAUFMANN
Hook	3X or 4X long, sizes **6, 8,** 10, 12		Hook	3X or 4X long, sizes 4, 6, **8, 10,** 12		Hook	3X or 4X long, sizes 10, 12, **14, 16**
Thread	Pale yellow 6/0		Thread	Hot orange 6/0		Thread	Hot orange 6/0 or 8/0
Tail	Bleached yearling elk hair		Tail	Light elk hair		Tail	Gray dyed yearling elk or deer hair
Rib	Fine gold wire, counterwound over body hackle		Rib	Fine gold wire, counterwound over body hackle		Rib	Fine gold wire, counterwound over body hackle
Body hackle	Light ginger, undersize		Body hackle	Brown, undersize		Body hackle	Brown, undersize
Body	Cream fur or synthetic dubbing		Body	Yellow fur or synthetic dubbing		Body	Bright green fur or synthetic dubbing
Wing	Bleached yearling elk hair		Wing	Light elk hair		Wing	Gray dyed yearling elk or deer hair
Hackle	Light ginger		Hackle	Grizzly wound over thorax		Hackle	Grizzly, wound over thorax
			Thorax	Amber fur or synthetic		Thorax	Amber fur or synthetic dubbing

4	Yellow Sally		5	Olive Sally		6	Little Brown Stone
Hook	3X or 4X long, sizes 12, **14, 16,** 18		Hook	3X or 4X long, sizes 12, 14, **16,** 18		Hook	3X or 4X long, sizes 12, 14, **16,** 18
Thread	Pale yellow 6/0 or 8/0		Thread	Olive 6/0 or 8/0		Thread	Brown 6/0 or 8/0
Egg ball	Red fur or yarn tag		Egg ball	Red fur or yarn tag		Egg ball	Red fur or yarn tag
Body	Pale yellow-olive fur or synthetic dubbing		Body	Olive fur or synthetic dubbing		Body	Brown fur or synthetic dubbing
Wing	Bleached deer or yearling elk hair		Wing	Gray dyed deer or yearling elk hair		Wing	Brown deer or yearling elk hair
Hackle	Ginger		Hackle	Blue dun		Hackle	Brown

Fishing Notes

Nearly all stonefly species crawl out of the water as nymphs, at dusk or after dark, before emerging into adults. You do not fish over hatches. Instead, you fish along the banks when the adults fall to the water or over riffles and runs during a late-afternoon or evening egg-depositing flight.

Whenever you see stoneflies crawling around in streamside vegetation, cast to the edge currents, no more than 3 feet out from the bank, being sure to probe up under brush, trees, and overhanging grasses. If masses of stoneflies take to the air, capture one, match it, and fish your fly to the splashy rises of the naturals.

To fish large salmon fly and golden stone imitations, rig your 5- or 6-weight with a leader the length of the rod, tapered to 2X or 3X. Cast upstream, along the banks or over rough water. At times, you can wade out from the bank and

Action can be explosive when you drop a stonefly dry over the head of a trout.

cast back in toward it, if the depth of the water allows. In this case, cast at an angle downstream, and feed slack into the drift. You're likely to set off a few detonations.

TRADITIONAL MIDGE DRYS AND THE GRIFFITH'S GNAT

The term *midge,* in older works, meant any trout fly size 18 or smaller. In current usage, it is the common name for aquatic insects in the family Chironomidae and any fly that matches them. Though most natural midges are small, some species, especially on lakes and ponds, can be imitated with size 10 or 12 flies.

Midges look and even sound like mosquitoes but do not bite. Mosquitoes live in marginal trout habitat; most midges live in prime trout water. Having a few flies that resemble them is critical to your fly-fishing success.

The simple traditional midge style consists of a tail, body, and hackle collar. The Adams Midge is an Adams with the wing deleted. It's the most useful of traditional midge dry-fly dressings, because it often takes trout that feed on midges of any color, so long as you use it in the right size. Because it's so simple to tie, I've also provided directions and photographs for tying the Griffith's Gnat, a dressing that represents a natural midge caught in the process of emerging.

Adams Midge	
Hook	Standard dry fly, sizes 18, **20, 22,** 24, 26
Thread	Black 8/0
Tail	Grizzly and brown hackle fibers
Body	Muskrat fur dubbing
Hackle	Grizzly and brown

ADAMS MIDGE
Step 1. Debarb the hook, secure it in the vise, and layer the shank with thread. Clip or strip five to ten grizzly hackle fibers from a web-free feather. Place them out of the way in your hackle pliers. Strip or clip the same number of brown fibers. Align the tips, and mix the fibers together by rolling them slightly between the thumb and forefinger of your tying hand. Measure them the length of the hook, and tie them in at the bend. Clip the excess.

Step 2. Twist a slender skein of muskrat fur onto the thread. Dub a body over the rear two-thirds of the hook shank. Select a grizzly and a brown hackle feather with fibers the length of the tails. You will use just four to five turns from each hackle, so they do not need to be the best feathers on the neck. (Other midge drys use just one feather; there it should be of high quality, for eight to ten turns of hackle.) Prepare the feathers by stripping webby fibers from the base. Pair them back-to-back, and tie them in at the end of the body.

Step 3. Wind the first hackle, taking just four to five turns, spacing them evenly from the end of the body to the hook eye. Tie the hackle off and clip or break off the excess tip. Wind the second hackle through the first. Tie it off. Clip or break off the tip. Hold any stray fibers back with a triangle formed with the thumb, forefinger, and middle finger of your off hand, and form a neat thread head. Whip-finish, clip the thread, and cement the head. Clear the hook eye before adding it to your fly box.

GRIFFITH'S GNAT
Step 1. Debarb the hook and fix it in the vise. Layer the shank with thread. Select an excellent grizzly hackle feather with fibers one to one and a half hook gaps, no more. Undersize is better than oversize on this fly. You need eight to twelve turns of hackle. Strip webby fibers from the base, and tie in the hackle at the bend of the hook, with the concave side toward you. Tie in two peacock herls about an inch from their tips, and clip or break off the excess.

Step 2. Twist the peacock herls and thread gently together, forming a herl rope. Wind this forward to a point just behind the hook eye. Let the rope untwist there, separate out the herls, and tie them off with a few turns of thread. Clip or break off the excess herl.

Step 3. Wind the hackle forward in closely spaced turns. Tie it off just behind the hook eye. Clip or break off the excess tip, gather stray fibers out of the way, form a neat thread head, and whip-finish the fly. Clip the thread and cement the head. Clear the hook eye. This fly is most useful in sizes 18 and smaller. If the eye is clogged with hackle, thread, or head cement, you'll be frustrated when you try to fish it.

Useful Variations

The traditional midge dry-fly style is tied in almost any color combination you can imagine. More than a thousand midge species have been identified, in many different colors, but the most common repeated themes—and therefore the most useful pattern variations—are gray, black, cream, and olive. If you run into trout feeding selectively on other colors among naturals, vary the tail, hackle, and body colors to match them. But try the generic Adams Midge first. It might just look right to the trout, even if its color is far wrong. You could also vary the color of the Griffith's Gnat endlessly, but the peacock and grizzly original will take fish when numbers of almost any color of natural midge get mired in the surface film.

The CDC Cluster Midge and Adams Cluster Midge represent midges hatching in great numbers and clumped together. They often gather on the water, and trout commonly take more than one at a time. The CDC or Adams Cluster Midge can be just as effective as a smaller dressing and is far easier to see.

1	2	3
4	5	6

1	Black Midge
Hook	Standard dry fly, sizes 18, **20, 22**, 24, 26
Thread	Black 8/0
Tail	Black or dark blue dun hackle fibers
Body	Black fur or working thread
Hackle	Black or dark blue dun

2	Cream Midge
Hook	Standard dry fly, sizes 18, **20, 22**, 24, 26
Thread	Cream 8/0
Tail	Ginger hackle fibers
Body	Cream fur or working thread
Hackle	Ginger

3	Olive Midge
Hook	Standard dry fly, sizes 18, **20, 22**, 24, 26
Thread	Olive 8/0
Tail	Blue dun hackle fibers
Body	Olive fur or working thread
Hackle	Blue dun

4	Griffith's Gnat
Hook	Standard dry fly, sizes 18, **20, 22**, 24
Thread	Black 8/0
Hackle	Grizzly, palmered over body
Body	Peacock herl

5	CDC Cluster Midge
	RENÉ HARROP
Hook	Standard dry fly, sizes **16, 18**, 20, 22
Thread	Olive 6/0 or 8/0
Hackle	Grizzly, over body
Body	Peacock herl
Wing	White CDC

6	Adams Cluster Midge
Hook	Standard dry fly, sizes **16, 18**, 20, 22
Thread	Black 6/0 or 8/0
Wings	Hen grizzly hackle tips
Tail	Grizzly and brown hackle fibers
Rib hackle	Grizzly, undersize
Body	Muskrat fur
Hackle	Grizzly and brown

Fishing Notes

Midge dry flies are almost always fished on smooth water in rivers and streams or on stillwaters. Midge hatches are important in lakes and ponds, spring creeks, and tailwaters, and you'll often need to match them there. You should fish such calm waters, and such tiny dry flies, with your most delicate gear. The leader should be long, with a 3- to 4-foot tippet of 6X or at times even 7X, though the large trout that often feed on these small insects will be difficult to capture once you've hooked them if you're using the kind of fragile tippets that fish the flies most effectively.

If you have difficulty spotting your tiny fly and following its float, try using the small fly as a trailer 4 or 5 feet behind a larger dry fly to let you know when you get a take. You can also slip a small foam or yarn strike indicator onto the leader several feet from the fly. Watch for any movement of the indicator, but also lift the rod gently to set the hook if you see a rise anywhere near it. The take will often be to your invisible fly.

Midge hatches usually happen on smooth flats in rivers. They're also very important in lakes and ponds.

GRASSHOPPER AND CRICKET DRYS

Grasshoppers and crickets often fall or are blown into the water by summer winds and are taken with enough regularity that trout become eager for their imitations. On hot days, a hopper or cricket dressing fished on a meadow stream or near the shoreline of a big river can cause an instant detonation, even when just a few naturals are around.

Hoppers and crickets have approximately the same body build. A dressing style that works for one can be tied in a different color to match the other. Most grasshopper drys are tied with yellow bodies, most crickets with black, but it's common to find hoppers in shades from olive to yellow.

Rather than list a single pattern style with a full range of color variations, I'll list the most complex tie, Mike Lawson's Henrys Fork Hopper, and follow it with a couple of styles that are easier to tie. No matter what style you choose, tie it in yellow and black, then watch for color variations in the insects on the waters you're fishing.

Henrys Fork Hopper
MIKE LAWSON

Hook	2X or 3X long, sizes **8, 10,** 12, 14
Thread	Yellow 6/0
Rib	Working thread
Body	Natural light elk hair, reversed
Underwing	Yellow dyed or natural elk hair
Overwing	Mottled brown hen saddle feather
Head	Elk hair, bullet-style
Legs	Yellow rubber legs, knotted

Step 1. Start the thread at the bend, and layer the rear half of the shank. Clip a patch of long elk body hair, clean fuzz from the butts, stack it, and remove all short fibers. Clip the butts straight across. Tie in the hair at the midpoint of the shank, covering the butts with thread. Gather the hair tips in your off hand, and spiral thread wraps back to a point just beyond the end of the hook. Take three to four tight turns of thread at what will be the end of the body. Spiral the thread back to the tie-in point.

Step 2. Draw the hair tips forward, surrounding the hook shank. Tie the hair off just in front of the midpoint of the shank, over the original tie-in point. Clip the excess hair tips, and layer them with thread. Spiral thread wraps back over the hair to the end of the hook, then forward again to the tie-in point, forming a segmented body with a bulbed extension beyond the bend.

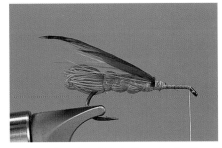

Step 3. Clip a few elk-hair fibers, dyed yellow if you have it, but natural is all right if you don't. Clean fuzz from the butts, align the tips, and measure the hair just beyond the end of the body. Tie it in and clip the excess butts. Measure a hen saddle feather to the end of the underwing, and tie it in at the same point. Treat several feathers in advance, either coating them with head cement or spraying them with artist's fixative, allowing them time to dry. End this step with your thread close behind the hook eye.

Step 4. Clip a patch of elk hair, clean all fuzz from the butts, and align the tips in your stacker. Measure the hair the length of the hook, and clip the butts straight across. Hold the hair around the hook in a pinch behind the eye, with the tips extending beyond the eye. Take several thread turns tight behind the hook eye, then secure the hair butts with tight thread wraps back to the wing base, capturing as many of the butts as you can. Don't worry about a few stray butt fibers.

Step 5. Gather the hair tips in your off hand and draw them back tightly, fully surrounding the hook shank. Tie them off with several turns of thread, forming a bullet head and at the same time flaring the hair collar. You can finish the fly at this point, omitting the rubber legs, and have a simplified and effective version. Just whip-finish, clip the thread, cut the hackle collar from the underside, and the fly is ready to fish.

Step 6. Clip two sections of rubber-leg material one and a half hook-shank lengths. Seat an overhand knot approximately in the center of each section. Tie one leg on each side of the body, the tips even with the hook eye, the ends kicking past the bend of the hook. Whip-finish the head twice before clipping the thread. Cement the thread wraps. Remove the fly from the vise, or turn it upside down in your rotary, and clip the hair collar fibers from the underside.

Useful Variations

The Henry's Fork Cricket is a bullet-head variation originated by Mike Lawson for the selective trout on his home stream, the Henrys Fork of the Snake River. It is a useful companion to the listed Henrys Fork Hopper and is tied the same way.

The Madame Xs in natural and black are simplified ties that fish very well for hoppers and crickets. The rubber legs are not natural but for some reason are very effective, though they're very ugly. It's not a secret that these same light and dark dressings will take large trout when golden stones and salmon flies are on the water.

Ed Shenk's Letort Hopper and Letort Cricket, developed for the fussy brown trout on his Pennsylvania limestone streams, are preferred flies where a lighter dressing is desired for a more delicate presentation. I recommend them especially for situations where trout are sipping the naturals rather than walloping them. To tie the spun and clipped deer-hair heads, follow the directions for the Muddler Minnow in chapter 5, but shape the head differently when you give the fly its final haircut.

Ed Schroeder's Parachute Hopper is the standard western hopper pattern in situations that call for exact imitation

1	2	3
4	5	6

plus extra visibility. Tie in the body, wingpost, and hackle, following the directions for the Parachute Adams on page 34.

1	Henrys Fork Cricket		2	Madame X		3	Black Madame X
	MIKE LAWSON		Hook	3X long, sizes **8**, **10**, 12, 14		Hook	3X long, sizes 8, **10**, **12**, 14
Hook	2X or 3X long, sizes 10, **12**, **14**, 16		Thread	Yellow 3/0		Thread	Black 3/0
Thread	Black 6/0		Tail	Light deer hair		Tail	Black dyed deer hair
Body	Dark brown elk, reversed		Body	Working thread		Body	Working thread
Underwing	Dark brown elk		Wing	Tips of head hair		Wing	Tips of head hair
Overwing	Black hen saddle feather		Head	Deer hair, reversed		Head	Black dyed deer hair, reversed
Head	Black dyed elk hair, bullet-style		Legs	White rubber legs		Legs	Black rubber legs
Legs	Black rubber legs, knotted						

4	Letort Hopper		5	Letort Cricket		6	Parachute Hopper
	ED SHENK			ED SHENK			ED SCHROEDER
Hook	2X or 3X long, sizes 8, **10**, **12**, 14		Hook	2X or 3X long, sizes 8, 10, **12**, **14**		Hook	2X long, sizes 8, **10**, **12**, 14
Thread	Yellow 6/0		Thread	Black 6/0		Thread	Cream 6/0
Body	Pale yellow fur or synthetic dubbing		Body	Black fur or synthetic dubbing		Wingpost	White calf body hair
Wing	Mottled turkey feather section		Wing	Dark goose feather section		Body	Golden-tan Antron
Collar	Tips of head hair		Collar	Tips of head hair		Wing	Mottled turkey feather section
Head	Spun and clipped deer hair		Head	Black dyed deer hair		Legs	Knotted pheasant tail fibers
						Hackle	Grizzly, wound parachute

Fishing Notes

Hopper fishing and, to a lesser extent, cricket fishing can be divided roughly into two different ways to fish the flies. The most common way to fish hoppers is to creep along the banks of a spring creek or meadow stream, watching for rises, casting short, setting the fly delicately to the water to float without drag into the window of a rising trout. Such fishing calls for 3- to 5-weight lines, long rods, and leaders 12 to 15 feet long, tapered to 5X or 6X.

The other method is to cast hopper and cricket drys tight to the banks of big rivers, usually from a drift boat or raft, often in wind. The line should be a 5- to 7-weight, the rod more powerful, the leader the length of the rod and tapered to 2X to 4X. It's usually best to place the fly on the water as softly as you can, given such strong gear. But there are many times, especially when the wind is up, that landing them with a smack attracts more trout. If your delicate presentation fails, even on the smoothest spring creek or tailwater, try setting the fly down hard. This might cause trout to attack it.

Grassy banks and frequent wind are typical of grasshopper-fishing situations.

CDC DRY FLIES

Olive CDC Caddis Adult

RENÉ HARROP

Hook	Standard dry fly, sizes 12, **14, 16,** 18
Thread	Olive 6/0 or 8/0
Body	Olive synthetic dubbing
Underwing	Light gray Z-lon
Wing	Medium dun CDC
Legs	Butts of wing fibers
Thorax	Olive synthetic dubbing

CDC, or cul-de-canard, which translates from French roughly as "butt of the duck," refers to the feathers surrounding the preening gland at the base of the tail of waterfowl. These feathers are fluffy, contain natural oils, and float high and well. When used as wings on dry flies, CDC feathers give the fly a posture that can only be described as touching lightly to the water. CDC dry flies are effective because many natural insects float exactly that way.

CDC flies fish best when tied for small insects that rest lightly and often briefly on the water before lifting off to freedom. That describes many small caddisfly adults, mayfly duns, and midges.

Rather than restrict the list to a single style for CDC drys, I'll list three styles that use simple and similar tying techniques and that represent those three major groups of insects. The CDC Caddis Adult, CDC Midge Adult, and CDC Dun are all styles originated by René Harrop, of St. Anthony, Idaho, a professional tier who stays on the cutting edge of fly pattern design.

CDC CADDIS ADULT

Step 1. Debarb the hook, fix it in the vise, and layer the shank with thread. Dub a somewhat portly body, as for all caddis adults, that covers two-thirds of the hook shank and tapers down slightly at the front rather than having a sharp shoulder. This gives a smooth base over which to tie in the wing. Clip a small bunch of gray Z-lon from the skein. Measure it to the end of the hook bend, and tie it in at the front end of the body. Clip the excess butts.

Step 2. Select a CDC feather from the package, gather the tips into a bunch, and measure them just a bit longer than the entire hook—bend, eye, and all. Clip the butts straight across at that point. If your CDC feather is a large and fluffy one, you can later gather the remaining fibers straight out from each side, thereby tying three flies from one feather. Measure the CDC wing to the end of the Z-lon underwing, and tie in at the end of the body. Do not clip the butts.

Step 3. Twist slender dubbing to the thread. Take two or three turns over the wing tie-in point, separating the wing fibers from the butts. Separate the wing butts equally out to each side. Take a single figure eight of dubbing between the separated legs to hold them in position, then two or three more turns of dubbing, tapering down to the hook eye. Make a neat thread head, whip-finish the fly, clip the thread, and apply head cement.

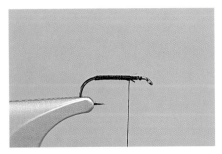

BLACK CDC MIDGE ADULT

Step 1. Layer the hook shank with thread. Peel a black ostrich herl fiber by running a rubber eraser against the grain several times. Tie in the stem at the bend of the hook, and use hackle pliers to wrap it forward to cover two-thirds of the hook shank. You can substitute a black biot from a goose or turkey wing flight feather for the body, and trout will not scold you.

Step 2. Gather the tips of a white CDC feather, or a clump of fibers from the side of a feather, and measure them the length of the hook shank. Tie them in at the end of the body, and clip the excess butts. They should stand just above the end of the body. Gather a small amount of black CDC fibers for the legs, and tie them in across the hook shank with three to four figure eights of thread. After they are secured, clip the tips to equal lengths on both sides of the shank.

Step 3. Apply a small amount of black fur dubbing to the thread. Take two to three turns of dubbing over the wing butts. Take one or two figure eights of dubbing over the leg tie-in point. Finish with tapered turns of dubbing down to the hook eye. Form a neat thread head, whip-finish once or twice, clip the thread, and cement the head.

Useful Variations

The most valuable CDC flies cover a narrow array of important midge, mayfly, and small caddis hatches. I'll list dressings for the most abundant color themes of each insect. Always keep in mind that you can vary the listed patterns in size and color to match any hatch you encounter.

Most caddis that emerge on quiet water, where you'll want to use CDC dressings, have either tan bodies and light brown wings or olive bodies and gray wings. Most mayfly duns that hatch where you'll want to use these flies have olive bodies and gray wings or sulfur bodies and pale gray wings. Many midge adults that you'll need to match have black bodies and gray wings or olive bodies and light gray wings. Carry the listed CDC dressings to cover these color themes, and you'll rarely be without the right match.

It's surprising how often the posture is more important than the color. If any caddis, mayfly, or midge is emerging, try a CDC dressing in the same size, even if the color is not nearly

right. Trout will often accept it with more assurance than they will a traditional dressing in the precise size and color.

| 1 | 2 | 3 |
| 4 | 5 | 6 |

1	Tan CDC Caddis Adult
	RENÉ HARROP
Hook	Standard dry fly, sizes 12, **14**, **16**, 18
Thread	Tan 6/0 or 8/0
Body	Tan synthetic dubbing
Underwing	Light gray Z-lon
Wing	Ginger CDC
Legs	Butts of wing fibers
Thorax	Tan synthetic dubbing

2	Black CDC Midge Adult
	RENÉ HARROP
Hook	Standard dry fly, sizes 14, 16, **18**, **20**
Thread	Black 6/0 or 8/0
Body	Stripped black ostrich herl
Wing	White CDC
Legs	Black CDC
Thorax	Black synthetic or fur dubbing

3	Olive CDC Midge Adult
	RENÉ HARROP
Hook	Standard dry fly, sizes 14, 16, **18**, **20**
Thread	Olive 6/0 or 8/0
Body	Olive synthetic dubbing
Wing	Light gray CDC
Legs	Light gray CDC
Thorax	Olive rabbit fur

4	Blue-Winged Olive CDC Dun
	RENÉ HARROP
Hook	Standard dry fly, sizes 14, 16, **18**, **20**
Thread	Olive 6/0 or 8/0
Wing	Light gray CDC
Tail	Light gray Z-lon
Body	Olive fur or synthetic dubbing

5	PMD CDC Dun
	RENÉ HARROP
Hook	Standard dry fly, sizes 14, **16**, **18**, 20
Thread	Pale yellow 6/0 or 8/0
Wing	Light gray CDC
Tail	Light gray Z-lon
Body	Pale yellow fur or synthetic dubbing

6	Gray CDC Dun
	RENÉ HARROP
Hook	Standard dry fly, size 12, **14**, **16**, 18
Thread	Gray 6/0 or 8/0
Wing	Dun CDC
Tail	Gray Z-lon
Body	Muskrat fur or gray synthetic dubbing

Fishing Notes

CDC dressings typically are most useful on smooth water, whether lakes and ponds or spring creeks and tailwaters, when trout are selective and fishing is tough. You'll need to use your most delicate tackle and tactics to fish them. Rods should be 8 to 9 feet long, balanced to 2- to 4-weight floating lines. Leaders should be 12 to 15 feet long, tapered to no less than 3 feet of 5X, 6X, or even 7X tippets.

Presentation techniques include the up-and-across-stream cast, the cross-stream reach cast, and the downstream wiggle cast. Take a position that lets you present the fly to feeding trout with the least disturbance and with a drag-free float.

CDC drys float well without dry-fly dressing, which will gum them up and sink them. Never use it. Carry a film canister of silica gel or a similar dry-fly desiccant. After catching a trout, resurrect the fly by shaking it in the canister to dry. If necessary, apply the special CDC oil available in fly shops.

Guides often fall back on CDC dry flies in heavily fished waters. For some reason, trout are exceptionally willing to take

Where insects hatch on smooth water, you will often fool more trout by going to an imitative CDC style of dry.

them. Add a dressing or two to your basic dry fly box, and see if they don't bail you out of difficult selective situations.

CHAPTER 4

Nymphs

Trout spend most of their time on or near the bottom, feeding on natural nymphs, larvae, crustaceans, and whatever else they can get in that rich and restful zone. They spend far less of it up where you can coax them to dry flies. If you'd like to increase the number of trout you catch, the best move you can make is to tie up an array of nymphs, then learn to present them to trout in approximately the ways that the naturals arrive.

SEARCHING VERSUS IMITATIVE NYMPHS

When trout feed on the bottom, they rarely feed selectively. Quite a variety of things drift on the currents down in the depths. Trout examine them all, accepting those that are living and nutritious and rejecting those that aren't. Most of your nymph fishing will be searching fishing, but it never hurts to select your fly based on the most abundant natural collected in the water where you're fishing.

Nymphs and larvae are the color of the bottom, or they would fail to survive. The first step in making up a basic selection of nymphs is to choose a few that cover nature's drab colors. To me, the basic four in a nymph fly box are the Gold-Ribbed Hare's Ear (brown), Dave Whitlock's Fox Squirrel Nymph (tan), the Herl Nymph (olive), and Polly Rosborough's Muskrat (gray). Your selection could be quite different, but it should cover the same basic set of colors.

Tie these basic flies in smaller sizes than you'd expect to be most useful. Most insects in the drift will be early instar mayflies, caddis, and even stoneflies that later would be much larger. If you insist on fishing size 8 and 10 nymphs because you think trout won't notice anything smaller, let me give you an easy assignment: Tie a size 16 or 18 nymph on a 10-inch trailer right to the

The Pheasant Tail (left) imitates blue-winged olive nymphs. The rougher Gold-Ribbed Hare's Ear looks like a variety of natural insects and is an excellent searching nymph.

A caddis larva of the free-living, or caseless, variety taken most often by trout.

hook bend of the larger nymph you're already fishing. See which takes more trout, and you'll soon have the faith that trout can see small flies down along the bottom. Tie most of your searching nymphs in sizes 12 to 16.

After you've covered the basic colors, add a few bead-head nymphs to your selection. It's not known whether trout are attracted to the flash or take the flies better because they get down deeper. What is known is that bead-heads catch trout when nymphs without beads do not. Start with the Beadhead Olive and Beadhead Fox Squirrel, and add others as you gain confidence in them.

After you've tied a narrow searching-nymph selection, begin collecting natural nymphs and larvae in your own waters, and tie a set of flies to match them. Don't tie precisely imitative *walkaway* nymphs; tie flies that give the impression of the living natural. Most nymphs listed in this chapter are tied with fur bodies because fur makes them look alive in the water.

WEIGHTING NYMPHS

A few nymphs will be fished just beneath the surface, imitating mayfly and stonefly nymphs or caddis and midge pupae, when trout are feeding on emergers rather than adults. These should be tied without weight.

At rare times, you might fish nymphs in the mid-depths, 1 to 3 feet down, to imitate nymphs or pupae on their trip to the top for emergence. In these cases, the nymphs should be mildly weighted.

Most of the time, you'll want to present your nymphs in the bottom zone. It seems that these flies should be heavily weighted. That's the old prescription, and it's still one way to do it. When you tie a fly, however, you usually won't know precisely how deep the water will be where you'll fish it.

I recommend that you underweight all of your nymphs. Use lead wire one size finer than the standard, which is the diameter of the hook shank. Such underweighting will let you fish the fly just beneath the surface. With a bit of line tending, you can mend the fly down

into the mid-depths. Add split shot to the leader, and you can fish the fly on the bottom.

NYMPH PRESENTATION

When you fish nymphs shallow, rig the same as you would with a dry fly. Use a rod 8 to 9 feet long, a floating line, and a leader 9 to 12 feet long tapered to a tippet in balance with the size of fly used. Because nymphs are heavier than drys, you'll use 3X and 4X more often than the finer 5X and 6X. But always go as fine as trout demand. If they are feeding visibly, present the nymph to them just as you would a dry fly. Let it drift to them drag-free. Watch the line tip for subtle movement, the trout for any movement toward the fly. If anything happens, set the hook.

Where the water is shallow and riffled, the old wet-fly swing works well with a nymph. Cast quartering across and downstream. Let the fly swing around on the current. Mend line to slow it if the drift is faster than a natural insect might swim. The same method works in the mid-depths, but you'll need a sinking-tip line to get the fly down.

The most effective way to fish the bottom is with the split shot and strike indicator method. You'll use this for most of your nymph fishing. Rig with the same long rod, floating line, and 9- to 12-foot leader you carry for all your other trout fishing. If it's a 5- or 6-weight line, that will help, but I do most of my nymphing with a 9-foot, 4-weight outfit, because that's what I'm armed with most of the time.

Fix the strike indicator two to three times the depth of the water up the leader. Use your tippet knot to stop the shot. Use two or three small shot rather than one large one. When the water depth or current speed changes, you can add or subtract shot to keep your fly in the bottom zone. The tippet should be just 10 to 12 inches long to keep the fly riding down with the shot. Experiment with a two-fly rig, one size 10 or 12, the other size 14 to 18.

Cast upstream into the current, 5 to 15 feet above the bit of bottom you want your fly to fish. Watch your strike indicator. If it hesitates, set the hook. Takes are usually subtle, rarely dramatic. Fish the drift out by drawing in line and lifting the rod as the fly drifts toward you, and by feeding line and lowering the rod after the fly drifts past you.

Lay the next cast a foot or so out into the current from the first. Paint the bottom with parallel strokes of the fly until you fish out the water or connect with a trout. Be sure your nymph is always on or near the bottom. The most common cause of fishless days with this method is failing to get deep enough. It's amazing how often you can cast over empty water for an hour, then add a single shot and discover the water is full of trout.

The best way to fish nymphs in most situations is with a split shot and strike indicator on the leader.

FUR NYMPHS

A few fur nymphs form the core of any successful sunk-fly collection. It would be hard to imagine venturing out to any trout water without Gold-Ribbed Hare's Ears and Dave Whitlock's Fox Squirrel Nymphs lined up in rows in my fly box. Like any of the best searching flies, they work so well because they are roughly the shape and colors of a wide variety of natural food forms.

Mayfly nymphs, caddis larvae, and other aquatic insects handle overcrowding, and also colonize new streambed areas, through *dispersal drift*. Once or twice a day, usually near dawn and dusk, a percentage of the population simply lets go and drifts downstream to new aquatic pastures—or to waiting trout. The greatest numbers of these insects that trout see in the drift are early instar nymphs and larvae: small sizes.

Tie your rough fur nymphs on standard nymph hooks, 1X long and 2X stout, usually in a narrow range of sizes, 12 to 16. Though the weight shown is standard, I prefer to underweight my flies with lead wire one size finer than the diameter of the hook shank.

Gold-Ribbed Hare's Ear	
Hook	Standard nymph, sizes 10, 12, **14, 16**
Weight	10 to 15 turns of lead wire
Thread	Black 6/0 or 8/0
Tail	Hare's mask guard hair
Rib	Oval gold tinsel
Abdomen	Tan hare's mask fur
Shellback	Mottled turkey feather section (omit on size 16 and smaller)
Thorax	Dark hare's mask fur, with guard hairs

Step 1. Debarb the hook and fix it in the vise. Wrap ten to fifteen turns of lead wire around the shank, centered between the eye and the beginning of the bend. Standard weighting calls for lead wire the diameter of the shank, underweighting for one size finer. Start your thread at the eye of the hook and layer it to the bend, using extra turns at the front and back of the lead wraps to form slightly tapered shoulders.

Step 2. Clip a small amount of hare's mask fur from the cheek. Remove most but not all of the underfur from the longer guard hairs. The tail should be rough and include some underfur. Measure the tail one-half to two-thirds the length of the hook shank, and tie it in at the bend of the hook. Layer thread over the tail butts to the back of the lead wire, and clip the excess there. Tie in 2 or 3 inches of oval tinsel behind the lead wire, layering thread over it back to the base of the tail.

Step 3. Clip fur from various parts of the hare's mask, remove most of the guard hairs, and mix it in a blender. Or you can buy hare's ear fur premixed. Twist a fairly fat skein of this dubbing onto the thread, slightly tapered from near the hook to the outer end. Wrap this from the base of the tail to just past the midpoint of the hook shank. The abdomen should be somewhat portly and far rougher than you would want on a dry fly. Take three to five evenly spaced turns of ribbing through the fur, tie it off, and clip the excess.

Step 4. Clip a section of turkey about one hook gap wide. Hold the section in place at the end of the abdomen with the thicker base end toward the hook eye, the marked side of the feather down. When brought forward over the thorax, the markings will then be on top. Secure the feather section tight back against the abdomen with thread wraps. If you don't, when you pull the section forward later, it will cause a gap between the fur segments. Clip the excess butts.

Step 5. The thorax should be darker, fatter, and have loose fibers sticking out to represent the legs of an insect. Blend a mix of hare's mask fur that includes more dark underfur than the mix for the body, and leave in most guard hairs. Twist a loose and fibrous section of this fur onto your thread, and dub it forward from the end of the abdomen to a point about one hook-eye length behind the eye itself. The fur should be slightly tapered down toward the eye.

Step 6. Pull the wing case forward, and tie it off just behind the hook eye. Clip the excess, form a neat thread head over the butts, and whip-finish the fly. Cement the head, and clear the eye of any fur, thread, or shellback fibers. If the thorax fibers are not loose and spiky at this point, use your bodkin point or scissors to tease out fur to the sides and the bottom, like legs on a natural insect.

Useful Variations

Since fur nymphs are prime in your searching-fly list, it's important that they cover the color spectrum of natural nymphs. The most prolific, and therefore populous, naturals blend in well with the backgrounds on which they live. That's why the most successful searching nymphs come in brown, tan, olive, gray, and black—the colors of vegetation and bottom rocks.

The Olive Hare's Ear is an excellent variation to carry if you fish lakes, or any moving water with lots of vegetation, where the naturals will tend to olive. My favorite searching nymph for rivers and streams is Dave Whitlock's Fox Squirrel, based on the large amount of luck I've had fishing that fly. The Hare's Ear Flashback adds a bit of flash to the original and often fishes better, especially in lakes and ponds. The TDC represents black midge pupae, which are so prolific in lakes that you should carry it if you fish stillwaters at all. The A. P. Black and A. P. Muskrat take a lot of small-stream trout for me and nicely fill out the color spectrum of fur nymphs.

Tie your fur nymphs rough, in the tapered form of natural nymphs and with a few hackle fibers or the thorax fur picked out to represent legs.

1	2	3
4	5	6

1	Olive Hare's Ear
Hook	Standard nymph, sizes 10, **12, 14,** 16
Weight	10 to 15 turns of lead wire
Thread	Brown 6/0 or 8/0
Tail	Hare's mask guard hair
Rib	Oval gold tinsel
Abdomen	Olive dyed hare's mask fur
Shellback	Mottled turkey feather section
Thorax	Hare's mask fur

2	Fox Squirrel
	DAVE WHITLOCK
Hook	Standard nymph, sizes 12, **14, 16,** 18
Weight	10 to 15 turns of lead wire
Thread	Black 6/0 or 8/0
Tail	Red fox squirrel guard hairs
Rib	Oval gold tinsel
Abdomen	$1/2$ fox squirrel fur, $1/2$ tan Antron, mixed
Hackle	Brown partridge (omit on size 16 and under)
Thorax	Red fox squirrel fur with guard hairs

3	Hare's Ear Flashback
Hook	Standard nymph, sizes 10, **12, 14,** 16
Weight	10 to 15 turns of lead wire
Thread	Tan 6/0 or 8/0
Tail	Hare's mask guard hair
Rib	Oval gold tinsel
Abdomen	Hare's mask fur
Shellback	Pearl Flashabou
Thorax	Dark hare's mask fur

4	TDC
	DICK THOMPSON
Hook	Standard nymph, sizes 10, 12, **14, 16**
Thread	Black 6/0 or 8/0
Rib	Silver wire or tinsel
Abdomen	Black fur
Thorax	Black fur
Collar	White ostrich herl

5	A. P. Black
	ANDRÉ PUYANS
Hook	Standard nymph, sizes 10, **12, 14,** 16
Weight	10 to 15 turns of lead wire
Thread	Black 6/0 or 8/0
Tail	Moose body hair
Rib	Copper wire
Abdomen	Black fur
Shellback	Moose body hair
Thorax	Black fur

6	A. P. Muskrat
	ANDRÉ PUYANS
Hook	Standard nymph, sizes 10, **12, 14,** 16
Weight	10 to 15 turns of lead wire
Thread	Gray 6/0 or 8/0
Tail	Moose body hair
Rib	Oval gold tinsel
Abdomen	Muskrat fur
Shellback	Moose body hair
Thorax	Muskrat fur

Fishing Notes

To rig a fur nymph for moving water, fix a strike indicator up the leader two to three times the depth of the water. Pinch one to three split shot on the leader, depending on the depth and force of the current. Make your casts short and upstream. Fish the drift toward you, mending and then feeding line so the indicator floats as a dry fly might. If it hesitates or dips under, set the hook quickly.

For lakes, I prefer a 10-foot sinking-tip line and fish these flies most often around the shallow edges or over visible weed beds, in 3 to 6 feet of water. Cast out, let the fly sink, then use a very slow retrieve. Trout will take gently.

Fur nymphs make great searching patterns when you want to cover a lot of water but have no indication precisely which fly might work.

HERL NYMPHS

Fibers such as peacock, pheasant tail, and even ostrich or marabou attract an outsize proportion of trout when they're wound as herl. Perhaps it's the minute points of light that each tiny barbule reflects or the way they quiver in the water. It's no secret that any fly tied with peacock herl for the body will wind up being a killer. For that reason, if not for its simplicity and the way it covers such a critical color—dark green—in the insect color spectrum, the Herl Nymph should be one of the basics in your sunk-fly box.

The Pheasant Tail is also a key fly in that box. I give the directions for tying it here because it is far more complex than the Herl Nymph. The Pheasant Tail represents nymphs of the prolific little olive (Baetis) mayfly group, so abundant in spring creeks and tailwaters. Originated by Frank Sawyer, riverkeeper on Britain's Avon, the Pheasant Tail has been modified by Montana's Al Troth to incorporate the deadly peacock herl.

Pheasant Tail	
AL TROTH	
Hook	Standard nymph, sizes 14, 16, **18, 20,** 22
Thread	Brown 6/0 or 8/0
Tails	Pheasant tail fibers
Abdomen	Butts of tail fibers
Rib	Copper wire
Shellback	Pheasant tail fibers
Legs	Tips of shellback fibers
Thorax	Peacock herl

Step 1. Debarb the hook, insert it in the vise, and layer the shank with thread. Select three or four long fibers from the center tail of a ring-necked pheasant. Measure the tips the length of the hook shank, and tie them in with thread wraps over one-half to two-thirds of the shank. Draw the butts back, and wrap a single layer of thread back over them to the base of the tail. When wrapped as herl, these butts will form the body of the fly.

Step 2. Clip 2 to 3 inches of fine copper wire for the rib. Tie it in at the base of the tail. Take thread wraps forward over the wire to the same point where you reversed the tail and body herl fibers. This will form an even underbody for the herl. Wrap the herl forward to cover the rear one-half to two-thirds of the shank. Tie it off there and clip the excess. *Note:* On hooks size 14 and larger, the tail herl might not be long enough. In that case, tie in separate herl fibers for the body.

Step 3. Select six or so fibers from the same pheasant tail feather that you used for the tail and body. Even the tips by pulling the fibers straight out before cutting them from the stem. Measure the tips the length of the hook shank, and tie them in protruding out over the eye of the hook. These will be reversed later to form the legs of the fly. Take thread wraps back over the butts of the fibers tight to the end of the abdomen. These will become the shellback.

Step 4. Tie in two or three peacock herl fibers at the base of the shellback. Wind them forward to a point about one full hook-eye length in back of the eye. You need to leave this slight gap between the eye and the end of the thorax to tie off the shellback, reverse the legs, and finish the head of the fly. Counterwind the rib forward through both the pheasant herl abdomen and peacock herl thorax. Tie it off and break off the excess by bending the wire back and forth.

Step 5. Draw the shellback fibers over the peacock herl thorax, and tie them off tightly in the gap between the thorax and hook eye. Clip the excess and discard. Be sure once again that you've left room for the head of the fly.

Step 6. Separate three leg fibers to each side. If you don't have that precise number, don't worry—trout can't count. Draw the far fibers back along the off side of the fly. Take one turn of thread over them to lock them in place. Draw the near fibers back along the near side of the fly. Take another turn of thread to lock them in place. They should slant back and slightly down. Form a neat thread head, whip-finish, clip the thread, and cement the head.

Useful Variations

The Flashback Pheasant Tail, tied in sizes 12 and 14, is an excellent dressing for lake and pond fishing. The Herl Nymph, Zug Bug, and Prince Nymph all incorporate peacock herl and are famous and effective flies. You should choose at least one of them for a central position in your sunk-fly collection.

The Pheasant Rump is a fine damselfly nymph imitation. When wet, its fibers mat down and it swims enticingly in the water. The Carey Special is a standard stillwater dressing for dragonfly nymphs.

When tying with fragile peacock, counterwind it with fine ribbing wire, as in the Pheasant Tail, to protect it from the teeth of trout so that they don't break the stems, causing your fly body to come unwound. In flies without ribs, twist the herl along with the tying thread before winding it. The thread will keep trout from breaking the herl. You can use standard weighting wire or underweight the listed nymphs by using wire one size finer than the diameter of the hook shank.

| 1 | 2 | 3 |
| 4 | 5 | 6 |

1	Flashback Pheasant Tail
Hook	Standard nymph, sizes **12, 14,** 16
Thread	Brown 6/0 or 8/0
Tails	Pheasant tail fibers
Abdomen	Butts of tail fibers
Rib	Copper wire
Shellback	Pearl Flashabou
Legs	Pheasant tail fiber tips
Thorax	Peacock herl

2	Herl Nymph
Hook	Standard nymph, sizes 10, **12, 14,** 16
Weight	10 to 15 turns of lead wire, optional
Thread	Black 6/0 or 8/0
Body	Peacock herl
Legs	Black hackle fibers
Head	Black ostrich herl

3	Zug Bug
	CLIFF ZUG
Hook	Standard nymph, sizes 10, **12, 14,** 16
Weight	10 to 15 turns of lead wire
Thread	Black 6/0 or 8/0
Tails	Peacock sword fibers
Rib	Fine oval silver tinsel
Body	Peacock herl
Hackle	2 turns of brown hen
Wing case	Wood duck flank, clipped short

4	Prince Nymph
	DOUG PRINCE
Hook	Standard nymph, sizes 10, **12, 14,** 16
Weight	10 to 15 turns of lead wire
Thread	Black 6/0 or 8/0
Tails	Brown turkey biots, forked
Rib	Oval gold tinsel
Body	Peacock herl
Hackle	Brown hen, undersize
Wings	White goose biots

5	Pheasant Rump
Hook	3X long, sizes 8, **10, 12**
Thread	Olive 6/0 or 8/0
Tail	Olive marabou
Body	Olive pheasant rump aftershaft feathers, wound as herl with the working thread

6	Carey Special
Hook	3X long, sizes 6, **8, 10,** 12
Weight	10 to 15 turns of lead wire, optional
Thread	Olive 6/0
Tail	Pheasant rump fibers
Rib	Gold wire, counterwound
Body	Peacock herl
Hackle	Pheasant rump feather

Fishing Notes

Herl-bodied flies are fished in an infinite number of ways, depending on the natural you're using them to represent. The Pheasant Tail is usually fished just before or even during a hatch of little olive mayflies. It can be fished just beneath the surface or as a dropper fly behind a larger nymph tumbled right along the bottom. The Herl Nymph, Zug Bug, and Prince, when fished in moving water, should be fished near the bottom. Present them with the split shot and strike indicator rig.

The Pheasant Rump and Carey Special are usually fished in lakes. Use a sinking-tip or full-sinking line, and the countdown method, to get them down. Fish them near the bottom or over weed beds, with a very slow retrieve. The Flashback Pheasant Tail is excellent in lakes when fished shallow during a mayfly hatch. Trout take the natural nymphs as well as duns during these hatches. Try dropping the nymph dressing on 20 inches of tippet off the stern of the dry fly you use for the same mayfly in the dun stage. When the dry dips under, set the hook.

Herl-bodied nymphs can solve situations where trout are feeding selectively or just feeding on the general run of drifting nymphs and larvae that arrive to them on the current.

FUZZY NYMPHS

E.H. "Polly" Rosborough, who passed away in 1997 at age ninety-five, first authored *Tying and Fishing the Fuzzy Nymphs* in 1965 (now in its fourth edition, Stackpole Books, 1988). Polly was one of the first to tie nymphs that captured not only the shape and color of natural trout foods, but also their critical movement.

The bodies of Polly's flies are tied with what he termed *fur noodles*. The dubbing is rolled into a long noodle, then tied in at the bend of the hook, captured with a thread loop, and rolled tightly so that the body, when wound, is segmented. If the body is not rough enough when finished, pick it out with your dubbing needle, a hacksaw blade, or a dentist's root canal tool. Polly did not weight his flies. At times I break that rule and underweight some of his dressings.

The Green Damsel is a standard pattern for the damselfly nymph to this day. It is also nearly unbeatable as a searching nymph when you arrive at a lake or pond and see no specific insect activity. Trout often bump into a stray natural down below and are usually eager to take an imitation.

Green Damsel
POLLY ROSBOROUGH

Hook	3X or 4X long, sizes **10, 12**
Thread	Olive 3/0 or 6/0
Tail	Pale olive marabou
Body	Pale olive rabbit fur noodle
Legs	Teal flank fibers dyed pale olive
Wing	Olive marabou one shade darker than tail

Step 1. Debarb the hook, place it in the vise, and layer it with thread. Gather a bunch of marabou fibers in your off hand, and peel or cut them from the feather stem. Hold the marabou with the butts near the eye and the tips well out beyond the hook bend. Tie it in with wraps forward over three-quarters of the shank. Reverse the butts, and take thread wraps over them back to the base of the tail. This lays a base for the body. Pinch the tail tightly half the hook length beyond the bend, and break away the fibers at that point.

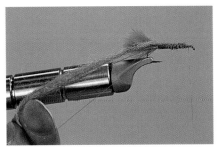

Step 2. Remove a substantial patch of dyed rabbit fur from the package. Coax the fur into a 2- to 3-inch skein in the palm of your off hand. With the palm of your tying hand, roll the elongated skein into a noodle. Tie in the noodle lightly with a few turns of thread at the base of the tail. Extend thread beyond the end of the noodle, capture the thread over your forefinger tip, and return the thread to wrap several turns around the hook shank, forming a thread loop. Run the working thread to the hook eye.

Step 3. With the thumb and forefinger of your tying hand, capture the tip of the noodle together with the end of the thread loop. Twirl them together until the fur and thread form a tight rope. It should be somewhat thick, slightly tapered from smaller at the base to thicker at the distant end, which will become the thorax of the fly. Grip the end of the rope in your hackle pliers.

Step 4. Wrap the fur rope forward in closely abutted turns, from the tail to a point about three hook-eye lengths—one-fifth to one-sixth of the shank length—behind the eye. Leave room for a long head, characteristic of Polly Rosborough nymphs. Twist the noodle as you wind it forward; each wrap around the hook shank untwists it one turn. Let the fur untwist after the last turn before tying it off and clipping the excess. This forms a tapered rather than a sharp shoulder.

Step 5. Select a teal flank feather that has been dyed olive, or substitute dyed mallard flank or partridge. If you do not have an olive dyed feather, run a green waterproof marking pen over a natural one. Select ten to fifteen fibers, align their tips, and clip them from the stem. Measure the fibers just short of the hook point, and tie them in with a soft loop on the bottom of the hook, at the end of the body. Clip the excess butts.

Step 6. Gather a substantial patch of marabou fibers from a feather a shade darker than the tail. Clip or peel them from the stem. Tie them in just above their butts, and clip the excess butts. Form a long and tapered thread head. Whip-finish, clip the thread, and cement the head. Measure the marabou wing one-third to one-half the body length, pinch, and break off the excess cleanly at that point. Rough it up before dropping this fuzzy nymph into your fly box.

Useful Variations

Polly's Near Enough is an imitation of the gray drake mayfly nymph *(Siphlonurus occidentalis)*. His Muskrat, in sizes 10 and 12, was originally tied as a cranefly larva imitation. Polly would wag a finger at me if he knew I tie it with weight, in sizes 14 and 16, and use it as a searching nymph.

The largest trout I've taken from my home Deschutes River intercepted a size 18 Muskrat rolled along the bottom, using the split shot and strike indicator method. It was a thick-bodied redside rainbow, and it fought hard in that brawling water. It weighed almost 5 pounds and had to be played gently on the fine-wire hook on which I'd mistakenly tied that fly.

Polly's Green Rockworm imitates riffle larvae of the prolific gray sedges *(Rhyacophila)*. His Casual Dress is a searching dressing that Polly speculated looks, to a hungry trout, like a drowned mouse.

Light and Dark Caddis Emergents are excellent during hatches of a variety of caddisfly species, especially fall caddis.

They represent the pupal stage, which trout likely take far more often than the more visible adult.

1	2	3
4	5	6

1	Near Enough
	POLLY ROSBOROUGH
Hook	3X long, sizes **10**, **12**, 14, 16
Thread	Tan 3/0 or 6/0
Tail	Mallard flank fibers dyed tan
Body	Gray fox fur noodle
Legs	Mallard flank fibers dyed tan
Wing case	Butts of leg fibers

2	Muskrat
	POLLY ROSBOROUGH
Hook	3X long, sizes 10, **12**, **14**, 16
Weight	Underweight or omit
Thread	Black 6/0 or 8/0
Body	Muskrat fur noodle
Legs	Speckled guinea fibers
Head	Black ostrich herl

3	Green Rockworm
	POLLY ROSBOROUGH
Hook	3X long, sizes 10, **12**, **14**, 16
Weight	Normal or underweight
Thread	Black 6/0 or 8/0
Body	Green wool yarn or rabbit fur noodle
Legs	Olive dyed teal flank
Head	Black ostrich herl

4	Casual Dress
	POLLY ROSBOROUGH
Hook	3X long, sizes 6, **8**, **10**, 12
Weight	Normal or underweight
Thread	Black 3/0 or 6/0
Tail	Muskrat back fur with guard hairs
Body	Muskrat fur noodle with guard hairs
Collar	Muskrat back fur captured in thread loop
Head	Black ostrich herl

5	Light Caddis Emergent
	POLLY ROSBOROUGH
Hook	Standard nymph, sizes 6, **8**, 10, 12
Weight	None
Thread	Black 3/0 or 6/0
Rib	Medium yellow thread
Body	Creamy yellow wool yarn or rabbit fur noodle
Hackle	Ginger hen, trimmed top and bottom
Head	Black ostrich herl

6	Dark Caddis Emergent
	POLLY ROSBOROUGH
Hook	Standard nymph, sizes 6, **8**, **10**, 12
Weight	None
Thread	Black 3/0 or 6/0
Rib	Orange thread
Body	Burnt orange wool yarn or rabbit fur noodle
Hackle	Furnace or brown hen, trimmed top and bottom
Head	Black ostrich herl

Fishing Notes

Fish the Green Damsel, Near Enough, and Casual Dress much as you might an old wet fly or streamer: with short strips of the line hand. The Muskrat and Green Rockworm, however, imitate naturals that do not swim; they should be tumbled along the bottom. They are excellent dressings for the split shot and indicator rig, though Polly did not fish them that way. I often use them to explore bright, shallow riffles where caddis and cranefly larvae abound.

Polly fished his Light and Dark Caddis Emergents unweighted, on floating lines, using short upstream casts and fast downstream retrieves in 2-inch jerks.

Each of Polly's dressings was tied as an imitation of a specific insect. All can be fished as searching dressings because they are based on food forms that trout see often.

Fuzzy nymphs are excellent wherever trout feed on nymphs, such as damselflies, that migrate toward shore to emerge.

RUBBER-LEG NYMPHS

For some reason, the addition of rubber legs, sometimes called rubber hackle, increases the effectiveness of certain nymphs. It's aesthetically unfortunate, because the resulting flies are ugly and also have far less resemblance to natural insects, which have an inherent beauty of form. But those creatures we're after, with brains the size of peas, declare them desirable, and we must always judge our fly-tying efforts through the eyes of trout.

It's possible that the movement of rubber legs in the water makes nymphs tied with them look more alive. It's also possible that the legs look like the protruding insides of a freshly killed insect. If you're a trout, I suppose that might make it look good to eat.

I'll give as a tying example the Yuk Bug, which is a killer, especially in streams with populations of salmon fly nymphs. The Girdle Bug stands on a par with it, in terms of taking trout, and is far easier to tie. Choose one of these ugly but effective flies for your basic-fly list.

Yuk Bug	
Hook	6X long, sizes 4, **6, 8,** 10
Weight	20 to 30 turns of lead wire
Thread	Black 3/0 or 6/0
Tail	Gray squirrel tail
Rib	Fine gold wire
Body	Black chenille
Legs	White rubber
Hackle	Badger, palmered

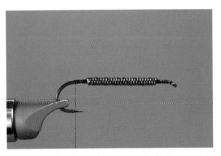

Step 1. Debarb the hook and fix it in the vise. Wrap twenty to thirty turns of lead wire the diameter of the hook shank. Don't underweight this fly; it's designed to be lobbed out from a boat and sink quickly along the banks or to be cast upstream while you're wading, to pitch abruptly to the bottom and bounce there. Start your thread and layer it the length of the hook, securing the lead with a slightly tapered shoulder at each end.

Step 2. Clip a small patch of hair from the tail of a gray squirrel, and align the tips in your stacker. Measure the hair half the shank length, and tie it in at the bend of the hook. Wrap thread over the tail butts to the back shoulder of the lead wraps and clip the excess. This forms an even underbody. Clip 4 to 5 inches of ribbing wire, and tie it in at the base of the tail. Clip 6 to 8 inches of chenille from the card, strip the fibers from 1/8 to 1/4 inch of the core threads, and tie in the chenille at the base of the tail.

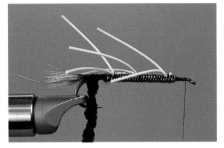

Step 3. Clip three sections of rubber legs, each about twice the length of the hook shank. Double the first section, and tie it in one-fourth the shank length in front of the tail. Tie in the doubled portion with a few thread wraps, then use two or three figure eights of thread to separate the legs. Don't worry about getting them in the correct position yet. Tie in the second set of legs at the midpoint of the shank and the third set one-fourth the length of the shank behind the eye.

Step 4. Wind the chenille body forward, using turns of the chenille to position the legs. Take a turn tight behind the rear set of legs, then hold the legs to the sides as you take another tight turn in front of them. Repeat the process with the middle and forward sets of legs. Wind the chenille to the hook eye and clip the excess. Select a hackle feather with fibers two to two and a half times the hook gap. Strip fuzzy fibers from the base, and tie it in at the eye of the fly.

Step 5. Wind the hackle back over the body. Because the body is so thick, you'll get just a few turns, even from a long hackle feather. Take one turn in front of the first set of legs, then one behind each set to the rear of the fly. Hold the hackle tip up after the last turn, and counterwind two turns of ribbing wire over the stem. Cut off the excess tip or twitch it forward against the wire windings to break it off.

Step 6. Counterwind the rib through the hackle to the head of the fly. The rib's purpose is to secure the hackle against the teeth of trout. Tie the rib off behind the eye of the fly, and clip or break off the excess. Make a neat thread head, whip-finish, clip the thread, and apply head cement. I normally use two whip-finish knots on this sort of fly, as it is designed to be brutalized by big trout.

Useful Variations

The Girdle Bug is simpler than the Yuk Bug and easier to tie. The simpler fly is used as much or more, and it might be the first rubber-leg nymph you want to tie if simplicity and speed appeal to you.

The Bitch Creek nymph is highly effective, but the weaving for the body is a bit complicated. Essentially you tie black and orange chenille sections in together, take a complete wrap of black, then hold it out to one side, wrap the orange up and over it, then back down and around, finally bringing the black to the same side, where the process is repeated. The orange winds up on the underbelly of the fly, the black on the back. The proportions and neatness matter little to trout.

The black and golden beadhead versions of Randall Kaufmann's stonefly dressings are not precisely like the naturals but at times are more effective than the same flies tied without rubber legs and beads. Deke Meyer's black and olive beadhead

rubber-leg dressings are just as effective in stillwaters as they are in rivers and streams.

1	2	3
4	5	6

1	Girdle Bug
Hook	3X, 4X, or 6X long, sizes 4, **6**, **8**, 10
Weight	20 to 30 turns of lead wire
Thread	Black 3/0 or 6/0
Tail	White or black rubber legs
Body	Black chenille
Legs	White or black rubber legs
Antennae	White or black rubber legs

2	Bitch Creek
Hook	3X long, sizes **4**, **6**, **8**, 10
Weight	20 to 30 turns of lead wire
Thread	Black 3/0 or 6/0
Tail	White rubber legs
Body	Black and orange chenille, woven
Rib	Gold wire over hackle
Thorax	Black chenille
Hackle	Brown, over thorax

3	Black Beadhead Rubber Legs Stone
	RANDALL KAUFMANN
Hook	6X long, sizes **4**, **6**, **8**, 10
Head	Gold bead
Weight	20 to 30 turns of lead wire
Thread	Black 6/0
Tail and antennae	Black goose biots
Rib	Black Swannundaze
Body and thorax	Black fur or synthetic dubbing
Wing cases	3 sets of mottled turkey sections
Legs	Black rubber legs

4	Golden Beadhead Rubber Legs Stone
	RANDALL KAUFMANN
Hook	6X long, sizes 6, **8**, **10**, 12
Head	Gold bead
Weight	20 to 30 turns of lead wire
Thread	Brown 6/0
Tail and antennae	Brown turkey biots
Rib	Gold Swannundaze
Body and thorax	Gold fur or synthetic dubbing
Wing cases	3 sets of mottled turkey sections
Legs	Black rubber legs

5	Black Beadhead Rubber Legs
	DEKE MEYER
Hook	3X long, sizes 6, **8**, **10**, 12
Head	Gold bead
Thread	Black 3/0 or 6/0
Tail	Black marabou
Legs	White rubber legs
Body	Black fur or synthetic dubbing
Hackle	Black

6	Olive Beadhead Rubber Legs
	DEKE MEYER
Hook	3X long, sizes 6, **8**, **10**, 12
Head	Gold bead
Thread	Olive 3/0 or 6/0
Tail	Olive marabou
Legs	White rubber legs
Body	Olive fur or synthetic dubbing
Hackle	Olive dyed grizzly

Fishing Notes

Rubber-leg flies were designed to be pitched to the bank from a moving boat or lobbed upstream and tumbled back down by a wading angler. Use a long 7- or 8-weight rod with a slow action. To fish these and other large nymphs from a boat, cast at an angle behind the boat, placing the fly within a foot or so of the bank. Let the fly sink a moment, then tighten the line and retrieve 4 to 5 feet before casting again. To fish these nymphs while wading, rig them with an indicator two to three times the depth of the water up the leader. You won't need split shot. Stand just downstream from good holding water. Cast short and almost straight upstream, then let the nymph sink and drift almost under your rod tip. Lift the rod as the fly approaches; lower the rod as the fly passes you and drifts downstream.

Rubber-leg nymphs are best when rolled along the bottom of big water or when tossed tight to the banks from a moving boat.

BEADHEAD NYMPHS

Olive Beadhead

DAVE HUGHES

Hook	Standard nymph, sizes 10, **12, 14,** 16
Bead	Gold
Thread	Olive 6/0 or 8/0
Rib	Yellow floss
Abdomen	Olive fur or synthetic
Thorax	Hare's mask fur

Beadhead nymphs attract trout in ways that standard nymphs do not. Many writers attribute their effectiveness to the extra weight of the bead, which takes them down quickly. I'd agree, except that you can weight the same fly with lead, get it down just as deep, and not get the same results in terms of trout caught. I ascribe most beadhead success to the resemblance of the beadhead to the flash many natural nymphs and pupae acquire when they exude a bubble of air between their outer and inner skins just before emergence. Or perhaps Gary LaFontaine, whose research involves skin diving, hit it when he wrote that beadhead nymphs have a jigging action that trout approve of. Whatever the reasons, they do work very well. If you haven't tried them yet, be sure to add one or two dressings to your minimal fly boxes. If you're like me, you'll depend on them a lot.

The listed Olive Beadhead is my own creation, one I tied some years ago because at that time I could find no olive dressing with a bead. Now there are others, but this one continues to be my favorite beadhead, based on success.

Step 1. Debarb your hook, and slip a bead around the bend to the eye before fixing the hook in the vise. If your bead is taper-drilled, place it with the narrow end toward the eye. Use extra small beads for hooks size 16 and smaller; small for sizes 12 and 14; medium for sizes 6, 8, and 10; and large for sizes 2 and 4. Use the bead size that slips around the bend of the hook without any straightening of the hook, which would weaken it.

Step 2. Layer thread on the shank from the bead to partway around the bend. Clip 3 to 4 inches of yellow floss. Separate out half of the strands, and set them aside for the next fly. Tie in the remaining half, starting down on the bend, and take thread wraps over the butts about half the hook-shank length. If you don't have yellow floss handy, you can rib the fly with yellow thread that is doubled or quadrupled.

Step 3. Dub a somewhat slender abdomen of green fur or synthetic, starting on the bend and ending just beyond the midpoint of the hook shank. Rib the abdomen with three to five evenly spaced turns of yellow floss. Tie off and clip the excess floss.

Step 4. Dub a thick and loose thorax, with some guard hairs sticking out to represent the legs of a natural insect. If the thorax dubbing is too tight when finished, use your dubbing needle to pick it out. Use plenty of fur on the thread, and take the last two or three turns of dubbing tight against the back of the bead. This fur, jammed behind the bead, holds it in place throughout the long life of the fly and the many trout it will catch.

Step 5. Make a four- or five-turn whip finish behind the bead. Use the thumb and fingernail of your tying hand to compact the whip and seat it securely behind the bead. Take a second whip finish directly over the first, and seat it with your fingernails before clipping the excess thread.

Step 6. If you're tying one of the many beadhead nymph variations with hackle or a shellback, your tie-in turns of thread form a collar just behind the bead. Your whip finishes become the outside layer of this collar and are not tucked in between the bead and the end of the body, as you would do on a fur beadhead nymph.

Useful Variations

Any nymph can be tied with a bead added to the head. Many will fish better for the addition. Most variations listed are standard nymphs converted to beadheads. They are all proven patterns. When a bead is added, the normal lead weight is usually omitted. Many anglers feel that when you add a beadhead to a nymph, you're no longer fly fishing. You'll have to make your own decision. I use beadhead nymphs and feel fine about it.

The Beadhead Prince is especially effective in tiny sizes, 18 and 20. The fly as listed is too intricate to tie so small. Abbreviate it by omitting all but the beadhead, the herl body, and the white wings. Such simplification works as well for smaller sizes of the other nymphs.

The Olive Beadhead Caddis Pupa is a style in itself and can also be tied in brown, tan, and gray. The Olive Beadhead Serendipity can also be tied in brown and copper, with Australian opossum rather than hare's mask fur.

1	2	3
4	5	6

---

1 Beadhead Gold-Ribbed Hare's Ear

Hook	Standard nymph, sizes 10, **12, 14,** 16
Bead	Gold or brass
Thread	Black 6/0 or 8/0
Tail	Hare's mask guard hairs
Rib	Oval gold tinsel
Body	Hare's mask fur
Shellback	Mottled turkey
Thorax	Dark hare's mask fur

2 Beadhead Fox Squirrel
DAVE WHITLOCK

Hook	Standard nymph, sizes 12, **14, 16,** 18
Bead	Gold or brass
Thread	Black 6/0 or 8/0
Tail	Red fox squirrel guard hairs
Rib	Oval gold tinsel
Abdomen	$1/2$ red fox squirrel fur, $1/2$ tan Antron, mixed
Thorax	Red fox squirrel fur with guard hairs

3 Beadhead Prince

Hook	Standard nymph, sizes 10, **12, 14,** 16
Bead	Gold or brass
Thread	Black 6/0 or 8/0
Tail	Peacock sword fibers
Rib	Oval gold tinsel
Body	Peacock herl
Hackle	Brown hen, undersize
Wings	White goose biots

---

4 Olive Beadhead Caddis Pupa

Hook	Standard nymph, sizes 12, **14, 16,** 18
Bead	Gold or brass
Thread	Olive 6/0 or 8/0
Rib	Oval gold tinsel
Body	Olive fur or synthetic dubbing
Hackle	Brown hen

5 Beadhead Pheasant Tail

Hook	Standard nymph, sizes 12, 14, **16,** 18
Bead	Gold or brass
Thread	Brown 6/0 or 8/0
Tail	Pheasant tail fibers
Rib	Copper wire
Body and Shellback	Pheasant tail fibers
Thorax	Peacock herl
Legs	Tips of shellback fibers

6 Olive Beadhead Serendipity
CRAIG MATHEWS

Hook	Standard nymph, sizes 14, **16, 18,** 20
Bead	Gold or brass
Thread	Brown 6/0 or 8/0
Body	Olive Z-lon, twisted
Thorax	Hare's mask fur

Fishing Notes

Explore riffles and runs 2 to 5 feet deep with beadheads, using the split shot and strike indicator method. Cast up into the current, and watch the indicator as it drifts freely downstream toward you. Cover all of the bottom with adjacent drifts. To give trout a choice, rig a beadhead with a smaller dropper, or use the beadhead as a dropper 10 to 12 inches off the stern of a larger nymph.

For shallow water, when trout are feeding on the bottom, rig a lone beadhead with a strike indicator 4 to 6 feet up the leader. Cast far enough upstream to give the fly time to sink. Watch the indicator for the slightest twitch. Another good rig is to drop a beadhead one size smaller than the dry fly you're using on a 20-inch tippet one size finer than that to the dry fly. This is my favorite combination for riffles, runs, and small streams.

Beadheads are excellent on any type of water when fish are not feeding selectively.

SCUD NYMPHS

Scuds thrive in lake and pond weed beds and in moving waters that are slow enough for aquatic vegetation to take root. You'll find their imitations necessary in most stillwaters, as well as many spring creeks and tailwaters. You will rarely use them in freestone streams.

Scuds are crustaceans and do not have the boom-and-bust hatch cycles of aquatic insects. They're in the water all year round. To find out if they're abundant in the water you're about to fish, merely lift a wad of weeds out of the water and watch what crawls out. If any scuds are revealed, use a scud pattern, unless some other food form is more abundant.

When scuds are preserved, they turn many interesting colors. That's why you see patterns tied for them in bright colors, including pink and orange. Those flies work, probably as egg imitations. But when scuds are alive, as trout see them, they are the color of whatever background they live upon. Usually that is vegetation, which is why the Olive Scud is the most important dressing you can tie to imitate them.

Olive Scud	
Hook	Curved scud, sizes 10, **12**, **14**, 16
Weight	Underweight
Thread	Olive 6/0 or 8/0
Rib	Tag of working thread
Tail	Olive dyed hackle fibers
Shellback	Clear freezer bag material
Body	Olive Hare-Tron
Antennae	Olive dyed hackle fibers

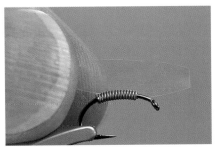

Step 1. Debarb a curved scud hook, and fix it in the vise. This is the traditional hook for scuds, but when swimming, the naturals are straight, so you can also use a standard straight nymph hook. Underweight the hook, using twelve to fifteen turns of lead wire one size finer than the diameter of the shank. Cut a shellback from a plastic freezer bag, one and a half to two times the length of the hook, the width of the hook gap or a little less, tapered at both ends.

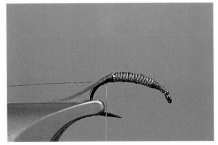

Step 2. Layer thread over the shank, locking in the lead wraps with shoulders at each end. Leave a 3- to 4-inch tag of thread uncut at the bend, for the rib. From a rooster or hen feather that has been dyed green, remove a substantial number of fibers, and measure them half the hook-shank length. If you lack a green neck, use a green waterproof pen to dye a white or light ginger feather. Tie in the tail well down on the bend of the hook. Clip the excess butts.

Step 3. Tie in the shellback at the base of the tail. Coat your working thread with sticky dubbing wax. Remove dubbing from the package, and rough it up into an elongated skein with your fingers. Stick this to the waxed thread, twisting just the ends to the thread to hold the skein in place. Catch the thread over the forefinger of your off hand, and return the thread to the shank, taking several turns there to form a dubbing loop.

Step 4. Twist the dubbing loop just enough to capture the fur into a loose dubbing rope. Don't wind it tight. It should have fibers sticking out in all directions. I prefer Hare-Tron, or some other mix of rabbit fur and Antron, for the combination of softness from the rabbit and sparkle from the synthetic. Wrap the body forward to a point just behind the hook eye. Leave room to tie off the antennae, shellback, and ribbing thread.

Step 5. Strip several fibers from the same olive feather you used for the tail. Measure them half the length of the hook shank, and tie them in just behind the hook eye. Clip the excess butts. Pull the shellback forward over the body, and tie it off at the base of the antennae. Clip the excess plastic shellback material. When tying flies for my own fishing, I confess to omitting the antennae most of the time.

Step 6. Take four to six evenly spaced turns of ribbing over the body and shellback. Be careful when ribbing to keep the shellback centered on top, capturing the spiky body material and directing it downward. Tie off and clip the excess ribbing thread. Form a neat thread head, whip-finish, clip the thread, and cement the head. Use your bodkin point or a dentist's root canal tool to pick out fibers on the bottom of the fly. The loose fur represents the myriad swimmer legs of the natural.

Useful Variations

Though live scuds come only in natural camouflage colors and turn bright only when they die, it's also true that scud dressings in pink and orange catch lots of trout. I list bright ones because they work so well. You should tie and carry one or two listed dressings in natural colors, but don't hesitate to tie and try those that are not found in nature.

The tan Lees Ferry Shrimp, originated by my friend Len Holt, was designed to match scuds living on gravel bars and stranded by the daily lowering of the Glen Canyon Dam tail-water, on the Colorado River in Arizona. When washed away as the water rises, these dead and desiccated scuds are taken eagerly by big trout.

Beadhead scud variations should not work, but they do. Try these flies in scud situations and also as searching dressings in waters where scuds are present.

1	2	3
4	5	6

1	Gray Scud
Hook	Curved scud, sizes 10, **12, 14,** 16
Weight	Underweight
Thread	Gray 6/0 or 8/0
Rib	Tag of working thread
Tail	Blue dun hackle fibers
Shellback	Clear freezer bag material
Body	Gray Hare-Tron
Antennae	Wood duck flank fibers

2	Lees Ferry Shrimp
	LEN HOLT
Hook	Standard nymph, sizes 10, **12, 14,** 16
Thread	Tan 3/0 or 6/0
Rib	Tag of working thread
Tail	Tips of shellback hair
Shellback	Tan elk hair
Body	Tan Antron, picked out
Head	Butts of shellback hairs

3	Pink Shrimp
Hook	Curved scud, sizes 10, **12, 14,** 16
Weight	Underweight
Thread	Red 6/0 or 8/0
Rib	Tag of working thread
Tail	Pink hackle fibers
Shellback	Pink Scud-Back or clear plastic
Body	Pink fur or synthetic
Antennae	Pink hackle fibers

4	Orange Scud
Hook	Curved scud, sizes 10, **12, 14,** 16
Weight	Underweight
Thread	Orange 6/0 or 8/0
Rib	Tag of working thread
Tail	Orange hackle fibers
Shellback	Orange Scud-Back or clear plastic
Body	Orange fur or synthetic
Antennae	Orange hackle fibers

5	Olive Beadhead Scud
Hook	Curved scud, sizes 10, **12, 14,** 16
Bead	Gold
Thread	Olive 6/0 or 8/0
Rib	Tag of working thread
Tail	Olive hackle fibers
Shellback	Clear freezer bag material
Body	Olive Hare-Tron

6	Tan Beadhead Scud
Hook	Curved scud, sizes 10, **12, 14,** 16
Bead	Gold
Thread	Tan 6/0 or 8/0
Rib	Tag of working thread
Tail	Ginger hackle fibers
Shellback	Clear freezer bag material
Body	Tan Hare-Tron

Fishing Notes

Scuds are fished most often in lakes or very slow parts of spring creeks and tailwaters. The naturals live in vegetation. Trout take scuds as they swim in or near the edges of weed beds or along the bottom. Scuds are slow and rather direction-less swimmers. They often pause to rest.

In water 2 to 4 feet deep, use a sinking-tip line. In deeper water, you'll need a 30-foot wet-head or even full-sinking line. To get the fly to the correct level, count 15 to 60 seconds as the fly sinks, and remember the count that either encounters weeds or catches a trout. Repeat the same count, and your fly will return to the same depth. Your retrieve should be a slow, short strip or patient hand-twist.

In moving water, fish a scud as the dropper with a smaller nymph, perhaps a beadhead, at the point. A strike indicator lets you get the fly deep and still know about takes when they happen. Add split shot if needed to get the flies to the bottom.

Scuds in both still- and moving waters live in weed beds. That is where trout will feed on them and where you will catch the trout.

STONEFLY NYMPHS

I'll step out onto a limb in this category and recommend that you tie nymphs only for the two largest and most famous stonefly groups—salmon flies and golden stones—and then only if you fish the western states and provinces. Goldens exist in nearly all streams in the West. Salmon flies are sprinkled in just a few famous rivers but are very abundant where they are found. If your waters have either group, you need imitations. Smaller stoneflies are important in the nymph stage only at rare times. You can imitate them with searching dressings you already carry, such as the Gold-Ribbed Hare's Ear or Olive Hare's Ear.

My favorite dressings for salmon fly and golden stone nymphs were originated by the late Charles Brooks, using a concept he called *tying in the round*. No matter which way his nymphs are tossed and turned by the currents, trout see the same thing. I use his Brooks Stone and Brown Stone as imitations wherever the naturals are abundant and also as searching patterns all over the world where they are not.

Brooks Stone

CHARLES BROOKS

Hook	3X or 4X long, sizes 4, **6**, **8**, 10, 12
Weight	25 to 30 turns of lead wire
Thread	Black 3/0 or 6/0
Tails	Black goose biots
Rib	Copper wire
Body	Black wool yarn
Hackle	Grizzly and brown hen
Gills	White ostrich herl, wound with hackle

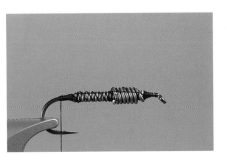

Step 1. Debarb the hook, fix it in the vise, and weight it with lead wire the diameter of the hook shank. Take a single layer from a point slightly in front of the bend to just behind the hook eye. Double it back in a second layer over the front one-third to one-half of the hook shank. Layer thread over the hook and lead, being sure to form slightly tapered shoulders at the front and back of the lead. This will keep your future yarn body from slipping off when you wind it.

Step 2. Select two black-dyed biots from the leading edge of a wing feather. Measure one biot half the length of the hook shank, and tie it in on the far side of the hook, at the bend, so that its curved side flares away from the shank. Measure the second biot the same length, and tie it in on the near side of the hook, for a forked tail. Clip 5 to 6 inches of copper wire and wool yarn. Tie them in together just behind the second layer of lead, and wrap thread turns over them back to the base of the tail.

Step 3. Wrap the body yarn from the base of the tails to the back of the second layer of lead wraps. Tie it off there, but do not clip the excess. This abdomen should be stout and slightly tapered. To achieve the taper, untwist the yarn so that the first few turns of it lie flat. As you go forward, twist the yarn to compact it. When wound, it becomes fatter toward the front of the abdomen.

Step 4. Select one grizzly and one brown hen feather with fibers one and a half to two hook gaps long. These should be fairly long feathers to execute two turns over the fat thorax. Use grade 2 or 3 rooster feathers if you don't have hen that's long enough. Strip webby fibers from the base of the stems, and tie in the feathers together at the end of the body, with their concave sides facing away from you, so that when wound the fibers will sweep back. Tie in two white ostrich herl fibers at the same point, and clip all excess stems.

Step 5. Wrap the thorax yarn forward to a point just behind the hook eye, and clip the excess. Leave room for tying off the hackle, gills, and ribbing, plus the thread head. Grasp the tips of the hackle fibers and ostrich herls together in your fingertips or hackle pliers. Take one turn forward from the tie-in point, one more turn halfway to the hook eye. Bring the tips to the eye and tie them off together. Clip the excess.

Step 6. Counterwind the ribbing the full length of the fly, and tie it off behind the head. As you wind the ribbing through the hackle, wobble it back and forth to keep from matting down any more fibers than necessary. The rib secures the hackle against the teeth of trout. Tie off the rib and cut or break off the excess. Form a thread head, whip-finish, clip the thread, and apply head cement. If the fly looks neat when finished, Brooks recommended grinding it into the dirt under your heel before fishing it.

Useful Variations

Almost all stonefly nymph styles are tied in two versions, one for the black salmon fly nymph, a second for the lighter golden stone. Both naturals have the same shape. The golden stone nymph is typically a size smaller than the salmon fly nymph: sizes 6 and 8 rather than sizes 4 and 6.

It's wise to recall that both of these groups are large when mature but have two- and three-year life cycles. The smaller first and second year-classes are in the water and available to trout in all seasons. That's why the same flies tied in sizes 10 and 12 are often effective when the largest sizes are not.

Randall Kaufmann's Black Stone and Brown Stone are analogous to the Brooks patterns fished for the same insects. Many of the most famous rubber-leg nymphs—the Girdle Bug, Yuk Bug, and Bitch Creek nymph among them—were originally tied as rough imitations for salmon fly nymphs. If you already have them in your minimum fly boxes, you might not need to add any further stonefly dressings.

| 1 | 2 | 3 |
| 4 | 5 | 6 |

1	Brooks Brown Stone		2	Kaufmann's Black Stone		3	Kaufmann's Brown Stone
	CHARLES BROOKS			RANDALL KAUFMANN			RANDALL KAUFMANN
Hook	3X or 4X long, sizes 4, **6, 8,** 10, 12		Hook	6X long, sizes 4, **6, 8,** 10		Hook	6X long, sizes 4, 6, **8, 10**
Weight	25 to 30 turns of lead wire		Weight	20 to 30 turns of lead wire		Weight	20 to 30 turns of lead wire
Thread	Brown 3/0 or 6/0		Thread	Black 3/0 or 6/0		Thread	Brown 3/0 or 6/0
Tails	Brown turkey biots		Tails and antennae	Black goose biots, forked		Tails and antennae	Brown turkey biots, forked
Rib	Gold wire		Rib	Black Swannundaze		Rib	Gold Swannundaze
Body	Gold wool yarn		Body	Kaufmann's Black Stone Blend or black fur		Body	Kaufmann's Golden Stone Blend or golden-brown fur
Hackle	Grizzly and brown hen		Wing cases	3 mottled turkey sections		Wing cases	3 mottled turkey sections
Gills	Light gray ostrich herl, wound with hackle						

4	Bird's Stone		5	Box Canyon Stone		6	Montana Stone
	CAL BIRD			MIMS BARKER		Hook	3X long, sizes 4, **6, 8,** 10
Hook	3X long, sizes 4, 6, **8, 10**		Hook	3X long, sizes 4, **6, 8,** 10		Weight	20 to 30 turns of lead wire
Weight	20 to 30 turns of lead wire		Weight	20 to 30 turns of lead wire		Thread	Black 3/0 or 6/0
Thread	Orange 6/0		Thread	Black 3/0 or 6/0		Tail	Black hackle fibers
Tails	Brown turkey biots		Tail	Black goose biots		Body	Black chenille
Rib	Orange floss		Body	Black wool yarn		Wing case	Black chenille
Body	Reddish brown fur dubbing		Wing case	Mottled turkey section		Hackle	Black, over thorax
Wing case	Mottled turkey section		Hackle	Furnace or brown hen		Thorax	Yellow chenille
Hackle	Furnace or brown hen, over thorax						
Thorax	Peacock herl						

Fishing Notes

Natural salmon fly and golden stone nymphs live on the bottom, usually in big and fast water. Trout find them tumbling along, tossed by the currents. Your nymphs should be fished in the same zone, with the same freedom. Rig with a floating line and a large, buoyant strike indicator at the upper end of an 8- to 12-foot leader. If the weight already on the fly is not enough to get it to the bottom, add split shot to the leader 8 to 10 inches above it.

Take your position downstream from the water you'd like to search, and make your casts short and upstream. Mend line and toss slack so that the indicator floats downstream without drag, much as a dry fly might. That is your best indication that the nymph on the bottom is drifting without hindrance. Make each cast a foot or two out from the drift line covered by the one before it, in this way covering the entire bottom.

Heavily weighted stonefly nymphs are designed to bomb to the bottom in the heaviest currents.

CADDISFLY NYMPHS

Caddisfly larvae come in two forms. *Casemakers,* the more abundant group, make cases of fine sand grains, small pebbles, and even vegetation. They crawl around on the bottom stones of streams and rivers or in weed beds of lakes and ponds. Trout take them, case and all, but not with regularity or selectivity.

The second group, called *free-living caddis,* live only in the currents of riffles and runs and carry no protective cases, though some make fixed shelters into which they retreat. These wormlike larvae are abundant in fast water and are knocked into the currents often. They're available to trout and at times are taken with some selectivity.

Most caddis nymph patterns imitate free-living forms. These include the listed Green Caddis Larva and its look-alike, the Tan Caddis Larva. George Anderson's Cream Peeking Caddis and Green Peeking Caddis represent cased caddis larvae with their necks, heads, and legs sticking out of the cases. The style is effective in fast and slow water, and even stillwater. Because they're so simple to tie, basic steps are provided for both styles.

Green Caddis Larva

Hook	Curved caddis larva, sizes 10, **12, 14,** 16
Weight	12 to 15 turns of lead wire
Thread	Brown 6/0 or 8/0
Body	Green fur or synthetic dubbing
Legs	Brown partridge fibers
Head	Hare's mask fur

CADDIS LARVA

Step 1. Debarb the hook and fix it in the vise. The proper hook has a curved shank and is called an English bait hook, scud hook, or caddis larva hook, depending on its use. All are the same. Weight the hook with twelve to fifteen turns of normal weighting wire the diameter of the shank. You'll fish these flies on the bottom. Start the thread at the hook eye, make a shoulder at the front end of the lead, take a few turns over it, then make another shoulder at the rear end of the lead.

Step 2. Twist dubbing onto the thread, from slender near the hook to fatter at the far end, for a tapered body when wound. Catch the thread over the end of your forefinger, double it back to the hook, then twist it tightly with the fur to make a dubbing rope. Wind this rope forward to cover the rear two-thirds of the shank, twisting the rope as you go forward, for a segmented body. Measure ten to twelve partridge fibers to the hook point, and tie them in at the end of the body, on the underside of the hook. Clip the excess butts.

Step 3. Mix underfur and guard hairs from various parts of a hare's mask, for a very spiky dubbing mix. I use this fur for so many flies that I shear several parts of the mask and mix the fur in a coffee grinder, then store it in a Ziploc bag for use at all times. Twist this fur loosely to the thread, and dub it from the end of the abdomen forward to the hook eye. Form a neat thread head, whip-finish, and clip the thread. Cement the head, and the fly is finished.

CREAM PEEKING CADDIS

Step 1. Debarb the hook and secure it in the vise. Weight it with 12 to 20 turns of lead wire the diameter of the shank. Layer thread from the eye to the bend. Tie in several inches of ribbing tinsel at the bend of the hook. Dub a tapered and fairly portly body forward to cover just a little more than the back half of the hook shank. This represents the case of the natural larva.

Step 2. Dub a short thorax at the end of the body. It should be just a couple of turns of soft cream dubbing, the same diameter as the forward end of the body. This represents the fleshy forward end of the natural insect protruding from the case. Measure ten to twelve brown partridge fibers to the hook point. Tie them in at the end of the thorax, on the underside of the hook, and clip the excess butts.

Step 3. Tie in two or three black ostrich herl fibers at the end of the thorax. Twist them together slightly, and wind several turns forward from the end of the body to the eye of the hook. Tie them off there, clip the excess tips, and hold the fibers back with your off hand while taking a few turns of thread in front. This forms a neat thread head and at the same time gets any stray fibers back out of the way. Whip-finish the fly, clip the thread, and cement the head.

Useful Variations

The Green and Tan Caddis Larva nymphs represent the most common colors of the free-living form. Use them in riffles and runs when no particular insect activity is obvious. Trout are always on the lookout for a tumbling natural caddis larva and will usually accept an imitation.

The Olive and Cream Caddis Midge dressings are Ed Koch patterns. Ed, who wrote *Fishing the Midge* (Stackpole, 1988), designed these tiny flies for selective trout on his home Letort Spring Run in Pennsylvania. They work well in situations where trout are taking small insects beneath the surface, whether caddis larvae or other food forms.

The Brassie takes trout in waters where small, cased caddis construct their homes from bright bits of sand and pebble. Chuck Fothergill originated the fly on his home stream, the Roaring Fork in Colorado, but the fly seems to work wherever trout and caddis are found together.

George Anderson, a fly-shop owner on the Yellowstone River, is one of the finest nymph fishermen on our continent.

| 1 | 2 | 3 |
| 4 | 5 | 6 |

His Cream and Green Peeking Caddis represent the cased variety when adrift, their heads and the foreparts of their bodies struggling at the front of the case.

1	Tan Caddis Larva
Hook	Curved caddis larva, sizes 10, **12, 14**, 16
Weight	12 to 15 turns of lead wire
Thread	Brown 6/0 or 8/0
Body	Tan fur or synthetic dubbing
Legs	Brown partridge fibers
Head	Hare's mask fur

2	Olive Caddis Midge Nymph
	ED KOCH
Hook	Standard nymph, sizes 16, **18, 20**, 22
Weight	Underweight or omit
Thread	Black 6/0 or 8/0
Body	Olive fur dubbing
Head	Peacock herl

3	Cream Caddis Midge Nymph
	ED KOCH
Hook	Standard nymph, sizes 16, **18, 20**, 22
Weight	Underweight or omit
Thread	Black 6/0 or 8/0
Body	Cream fur dubbing
Head	Peacock herl

4	Brassie
	CHUCK FOTHERGILL
Hook	Standard nymph, sizes 14, **16, 18**, 20
Thread	Black 6/0 or 8/0
Body	Copper wire
Head	Peacock herl

5	Cream Peeking Caddis
	GEORGE ANDERSON
Hook	2X long, sizes **10, 12**, 14, 16
Weight	12 to 20 turns of lead wire
Thread	Black 6/0 or 8/0
Rib	Oval gold tinsel
Abdomen	Dark hare's mask fur
Thorax	Cream fur or synthetic
Legs	Brown partridge fibers
Head	Black ostrich herl

6	Green Peeking Caddis
	GEORGE ANDERSON
Hook	2X long, sizes **10, 12**, 14, 16
Weight	12 to 20 turns of lead wire
Thread	Black 6/0 or 8/0
Rib	Oval gold tinsel
Abdomen	Dark hare's mask fur
Thorax	Bright green fur or synthetic
Legs	Brown partridge fibers
Head	Black ostrich herl

Fishing Notes

With the exception of the Olive and Cream Caddis Midge Nymphs, all of these caddis larva dressings are designed to be fished tumbling along the bottom, usually in riffles or runs. If the fly has enough inherent weight to get to the bottom, rig a strike indicator two to three times the depth of the water above it on the leader. If needed, add split shot to get it down. Cast upstream, short, and fish the nymph back down toward you.

Ed Koch's midge nymphs are fished most often to sighted and feeding trout, active along the banks or near weed beds in spring creeks and tailwaters, usually in 1 to 3 feet of water with modest current. Rig with a 12- to 15-foot leader and 2 to 3 feet of 5X, 6X, or even 7X tippet. Cast well above a sighted trout, both to avoid spooking it and to give the fly time to sink to the level at which the fish is feeding. Add a tiny yarn strike indicator 4 to 6 feet up the leader from the fly to let you know about the very subtle takes you'll get in this kind of fishing.

Free-living caddis larvae are especially abundant in the riffles of freestone streams. Flies tied to resemble them make excellent imitations and good searching flies as well.

SERENDIPITY NYMPHS

These were the serendipitous discovery of the late Ross Marigold, beloved guide on the Madison River for many years. Ross tied the originals with yarn, in bright colors, twisted tightly to form segmented bodies. Z-lon is now the accepted body material, but the goal is still a tight, segmented effect, which can still be achieved with wool and synthetic yarns. I use Z-lon, Antron yarn, or Microcable, which is constructed with a lead wire core so that the fly is inherently weighted.

The Serendipity style is similar to the old British Buzzer, tied for midge pupae and designed to fish in or near the surface film. The deer-hair head of a Buzzer is left long and dressed with floatant to achieve this effect. On this continent, the Serendipity is tied most often with the head clipped short. The fly is then fished on or near the bottom, often in tandem with a larger nymph. It looks strikingly like a small caddis or midge larva or pupa, and it's likely trout take it for one of them. It's also probable that trout take Serendipities simply because they look alive and like something good to eat.

Olive Serendipity	
Hook	Curved scud, sizes 14, **16, 18,** 20
Thread	Tan 6/0 or 8/0
Body	Olive Z-lon, Antron yarn, or Microcable
Head	Deer body hair, spun and clipped

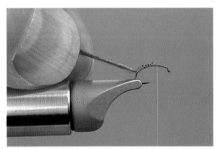

Step 1. Debarb the hook and fix it in the vise. Layer the shank with thread well down around the bend. Clip a 3- to 5-inch section of Z-lon, yarn, or Microcable. Z-lon, the standard, is shown here. Tie it in tightly on the bend of the hook, and wrap thread turns forward over it to a point about one-fourth the shank length behind the eye before clipping the excess. This forms an even base for the body.

Step 2. Twist the Z-lon or yarn in your fingers to form a tight rope. If you're using Microcable, it's not necessary to twist it. After twisting the body material, capture the end in your hackle pliers. Wind the body forward in tight, adjacent turns. Twist the rope one turn for each wrap forward, or it will untwist and relax, and you won't get the segmentation you're after. To form a less abrupt shoulder, let the last turn untwist before tying it off. Clip the excess.

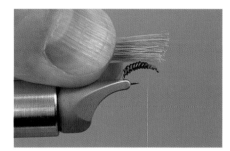

Step 3. Clip a small clump of deer hair from the hide. Clean fuzzy underfur from the hair butts, and trim the butts straight across. Reverse the hair in your fingers, and clip off the tips so the remaining hair is about 1/2 inch long.

Step 4. Center the hair in the gap between the end of the body and the hook eye, and work it down around the hook shank on both sides. Take two soft loops around the hair without drawing either tight. Let go of the pinch on the hair, at the same time drawing both loops tight around the hair, flaring it. Work several more turns of thread forward through the hair to the hook eye. Use the nails of your tying-hand thumb and forefinger to force hair back away from the eye. Whip-finish the head and clip the thread.

Step 5. You can give the fly what amounts to a crew cut or clip it Buzzer style. The most common way to tie the fly for use in the United States and Canada is to clip it tight across the bottom, on both sides, then across the top, and finish by clipping the hair short on the back side of the head. I prefer to clip the head Buzzer style, however, because the long hair can always be shortened on the stream or lake with a single nip of your leader clippers if you want to fish it in or near the surface film.

Alternate Step 5. To form the head Buzzer style, especially for use during midge hatches on the smooth parts of streams or on any lake or pond, leave the hairs at the back of the head long. Take a single tight cut on the bottom, another tight cut on either side, then a cut angled back on top of the head, leaving a few hairs sticking out the back. Clip these about half the length of the body, and the fly is finished. Dress this topknot with floatant, and the fly will suspend from the surface film, just like a natural midge pupa.

Useful Variations

The most useful variations of the Serendipity cover the common color themes of natural midges and other small insects, including light olive, red, brown, and black. I highly recommend the Olive, Black, and Red Serendipities for prominent positions in any minimalist set of fly boxes. They match maddening hatches of midges that are difficult to solve with any other type of fly. They're also excellent whenever trout seem to be feeding on anything small or for those times when it's advantageous to drop a tiny fly off the hook bend of a larger nymph and tumble the pair of them along the bottom.

Red and Black Beadhead Serendipities are the two colors I use most often with the brightness of a beadhead added. The Olive Beadhead version is listed in the section on beadhead nymphs. You can tie either the standard or beadhead variation in any color for which you can find Z-lon, Antron yarn, or Microcable. All will work. Just keep in mind that you can't fish the beadhead versions in or near the surface film.

1	2	3
4	5	6

1	Light Olive Serendipity
Hook	Curved scud, sizes 14, **16, 18,** 20
Thread	Tan 6/0 or 8/0
Body	Light olive Z-lon, Antron yarn, or Microcable
Head	Deer body hair, spun and clipped

2	Red Serendipity
Hook	Curved scud, sizes 14, **16, 18,** 20
Thread	Tan 6/0 or 8/0
Body	Red Z-lon, Antron yarn, or Microcable
Head	Deer body hair, spun and clipped

3	Brown Serendipity
Hook	Curved scud, sizes 14, **16, 18,** 20
Thread	Tan 6/0 or 8/0
Body	Brown Z-lon, Antron yarn, or Microcable
Head	Deer body hair, spun and clipped

4	Black Serendipity
Hook	Curved scud, sizes 14, **16, 18,** 20
Thread	Tan 6/0 or 8/0
Body	Black Z-lon, Antron yarn, or Microcable
Head	Deer body hair, spun and clipped

5	Red Beadhead Serendipity
Hook	Curved scud, sizes 14, **16, 18,** 20
Bead	Gold or brass
Thread	Brown 6/0 or 8/0
Body	Red Z-lon, Antron yarn, or Microcable
Thorax	Hare's mask fur

6	Black Beadhead Serendipity
Hook	Curved scud, sizes 14, **16, 18,** 20
Bead	Gold or brass
Thread	Tan 6/0 or 8/0
Body	Black Z-lon, Antron yarn, or Microcable
Thorax	Hare's mask fur

Fishing Notes

Serendipities, like most tiny nymphs, can be fished in a variety of ways. I frequently drop one on a 20-inch tippet tied to the bend of the dry fly I'm using at the time. This works especially well during midge hatches and for fish sipping selectively in eddies. I also drop the smaller fly on a 1-foot tippet behind a heavily weighted salmon fly nymph, or paired with a scud nymph rigged with split shot and a strike indicator, to fish the bottom.

In shallow spring creeks and tailwaters, trout often feed on tiny nymphs drifting along or just above the bottom. If you can see the fish working, try tying a Serendipity to a long, fine tippet. Tie a tiny yarn indicator 4 to 8 feet up the leader. Present the nymph as delicately as you would a dry fly, far enough upstream from the working trout that the fly has time to sink to the trout's level. This works well with Beadhead Serendipities because they sink at a sure rate.

To fish a Serendipity in stillwater, use a floating line and dress your leader to within a foot of the fly. This will help it hang in or near the surface film. Let it sit there. Set the hook

Ross Marigold originated the Serendipity nymphs to resemble tiny nymphs and larvae on his home Madison River in Montana.

when you see a swirl in the area. The trout you catch will often be outsize for the fragile tippet you must use to fish the flies correctly in this manner. Hang on. Good luck.

CHAPTER 5

Wet Flies and Streamers

In this imitative age, wet flies and streamers are considered by most sophisticated anglers to be no more than archaic attractor flies. It's true that many are tied to be bright and in truth resemble nothing in nature. But even these catch trout at times, and a few of them have value in your basic array of trout flies.

If you think about trout food forms, and then tie wet flies and streamers that look a lot like them, you can tie a narrow range of patterns that carry even greater value in any list of essential trout flies.

SEARCHING VERSUS IMITATIVE WET FLIES AND STREAMERS

The fact that the best searching flies are almost always based on some common trout food form still holds true for wet flies and streamers, though the connection is at times less obvious than it is with flies based on insects that you can collect, observe, and match.

Wet flies represent, most often in an impressionistic way, the transitional stages of the same insects you would match at an earlier stage with a nymph or at a later stage with a dry fly. As a prime example, look at the caddisfly. In the larval stage, it lives on the bottom, either in a case or in the more succulent free-living form. You imitate it with a nymph. In the adult stage, the caddis floats on the surface briefly, and you imitate it with a dry fly. Most caddis that get eaten by trout, however, are taken in a couple of hidden stages that are more difficult to observe.

Larval caddis, when they reach full growth, retreat into cases or shelters and transform into pupae. When ready for emergence, these pupae escape from the case or shelter and swim to the top, where the adult quickly pops free and flies away. Trout take more pupae than they do adults during an emergence, and they feed on the concentrated pupae more selectively than they ever do on the scattered larvae.

The second hidden stage of the caddis is the adult itself. The majority of stream species dive beneath the surface, swim to the bottom, and lay their eggs there. Most caddis adults that get eaten by trout are taken during that hidden swim toward the bottom rather than off the surface itself. In both pupal and swimming adult stages, the natural insect is best matched with a wet fly, not a nymph or dry.

Once you've made that connection and switched to a wet, your fly can be a rough approximation of the pupae or adults the trout are taking rather than an exact imitation. If you capture a natural and choose an imitation, that won't hurt. Most of the time, though, if you choose a fly that is the right size and approximate right color, it will take trout. That's why most of the wet flies listed in this chapter are in nature's repeated color themes but aren't tied as exact imitations.

The same applies roughly to streamers. The most famous, the Muddler Minnow, was originated as an imitation of the sculpin. It is highly successful because that bottom-dwelling baitfish and many others like it are widespread and attractive to trout. The Muddler is one of the most effective searching flies you can fish simply because it reminds so many trout of something good to eat, even if they haven't chased one down and eaten it recently.

Wet flies are still the best style of fly to imitate caddis pupae on their way to the surface for emergence.

The three primary styles of wet flies are (from left) soft-hackles, flymphs, and traditional winged wets.

The Olive Woolly Bugger and the leech that it imitates.

Other streamers, such as the Mickey Finn, resemble more streamlined minnows. Woolly Buggers resemble everything from pollywogs to dragonfly and damselfly nymphs, though they were originally tied to represent leeches. Again, it's the number of things a trout can mistake them for that makes them so valuable in your collection of essential trout flies.

PRESENTATION OF WET FLIES AND STREAMERS

The most common method for fishing wet flies and streamers is the down-and-across-stream swing. Rigging is normally with a floating line and a leader a little longer than the length of the rod. The cast is made quartering across the current. The fly is given a few feet of its drift to sink, then coaxed into swimming downstream and across the current, until it comes to a stop almost directly downstream from the rod.

Many modern writers denigrate this method as mere "chuck-and-chance-it," although it's extremely effective in water that's somewhat shallow, say 2 to 4 feet deep, and with moderate to brisk flow. It's not difficult to understand why. Many natural insects, from caddis pupae and adults to mayfly nymphs and drowned duns, drift at the whim of the currents and are roughly represented by swinging wet flies. And nothing looks more like a baitfish out for a swim than a streamer fished on the swing across the current.

This cross-stream swing can be given some depth either by casting higher into the current to give the fly more time to sink or by rigging with a sinking-tip line. The method can be improved upon by mending line to slow the swing, if the fly is moving too fast, or by feeding line to increase the downstream belly of the line, and therefore speed the swing, if the fly is moving too slowly.

Wet flies are at times more effective than drys when fished with an upstream, dead-drift presentation to rising trout. This is especially true when trout are feeding on emergers. A wet fly can be dressed with floatant and fished in the surface film, or you can leave it undressed and it will sink a few inches and ride back toward you just beneath the surface film.

Your choice, dressed or undressed, should be based on your observance of the rise. If a bubble is left in it, this means that the trout broke the surface and took something on or in the surface film, and you should fish the wet fly dressed so it floats flush in the film. If there is no bubble, the trout fed so close to the surface that the rise rings broke up to it, and you should fish the fly without floatant so that it sinks just inches.

It's often most effective to bounce a streamer right along the bottom. Unlike a nymph, however, which is allowed to merely tumble along, the streamer should appear to be swimming at least feebly. This method is best employed with a streamer that is moderately weighted or, if the water is deeper than 5 feet and the current at all fast, heavily weighted. Choose a line with a sink rate that will tug the fly down in the water type where you're fishing.

Make the cast at an angle across and upstream rather than across and down. Mend line and give the fly lots of time to sink. When you feel it's on or near the bottom, let the current first put a slight belly into your line, then swing the fly around and downstream. Animating the fly with a rhythmic rocking of the rod tip will cause the fly to swim and rest as it ambles along the bottom. That can help entice takes.

When fishing lakes and ponds with wet flies and streamers, your first concern should be the depth at which the flies are presented. In almost all cases, you should fish near the bottom or just above weed beds. The bottom or weeds will be at different depths in different places. Choose a line type that will get the fly down, from a floater for very shallow water, to a sinking-tip for water 3 to 5 feet deep, to a fast-sinking wet-head for water 6 to 10 feet deep, to an ultrafast-sinking Shooting Head where the water is deeper than that.

Many hatches that look like dry-fly situations are actually better when fished with wet flies, because the naturals, such as this mass of caddis, are taken by trout while swimming down to the bottom to lay their eggs.

Use the countdown method to get the fly down deep enough and also to ensure that you can repeat your presentation if a fish takes the fly. Trout in stillwaters tend to travel in pods. If you hook one, returning to the same depth and repeating the same retrieve—usually a slow strip or hand-twist—will often produce further action.

SOFT-HACKLED WET FLIES

Simple soft-hackled wets were first tied more than a century ago for hill-stream trout in the border region of Scotland and England. They were tied using sewing basket silks and the feathers from an occasional poached partridge or other land bird. That's all the tiers had available, and they made it work. Sylvester Nemes, in his brilliant book *The Soft-Hackled Fly* (Stackpole Books, 1975), brought these flies to the attention of American anglers. His flies, and the basic methods he uses to fish them, take trout well to this day.

Soft-hackled wet flies resemble many winged insect types—mayflies, caddis, and stoneflies—that have drowned and become disheveled. The naturals are tossed at the whim of the current. The soft fibers of these wet flies open and close, kick, and all but scream that they're alive and good to eat to a trout.

The listed Grouse & Orange, along with the Partridge & Yellow and Partridge & Green, all tied in sizes 12 and 14, cover many fishing situations. Two ways to tie them are demonstrated here.

Grouse & Orange

Hook	Standard wet fly, sizes 10, **12, 14,** 16
Thread	Orange Pearsall's Gossamer silk or 6/0
Hackle	Grouse wing shoulder feather
Body	Working silk or orange floss
Thorax	Hare's mask fur

METHOD 1

Step 1. Wax the first inch of tying silk with beeswax. Start the thread just behind the hook eye, and clip the excess tag. From the shoulder of a grouse wing, select a partridge feather with fibers about two hook gaps long. Prepare the feather by stripping fuzzy fibers from the base, then flaring all but the short tip fibers to 90-degree angles to the stem. Hold the feather by the stem, with the concave side toward you, and peel away the top fibers. Tie in the feather at the hook eye, with the tip out over the eye, and clip the stem.

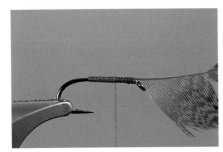

Step 2. Wind tightly adjacent turns of silk to a point on the shank just past the hook point. Take a second layer of silk in tightly abutted wraps forward over the first to a point one-third the shank length behind the eye. This short body becomes an undercolor to the hackle as the hackle fibers open and close around the body. If you were to use just a single layer of silk thread, or two layers of 6/0 thread, the dark color of the hook would come through and kill the color of the body as soon as the fly got wet.

Step 3. Wax 1 to 2 inches of thread with sticky dubbing wax. Twist a short bit of hare's mask fur dubbing, with some guard hairs mixed in, onto the waxed thread. It should be loose and fibrous. Take four to six turns of dubbing just behind the hackle tie-in point, covering one-fourth to one-third of the shank. This serves to make the fly look buggy, but its main purpose is to prop the hackle and make it more active as it opens and closes in the water.

Step 4. End Step 3 with your silk thread behind the hackle. Grasp the hackle tip in your hackle pliers. Take one turn of hackle at the hook eye, then a second turn behind it, ending tight against the fur thorax. Hold the hackle tip up, and catch it with two turns of thread over the stem. Cut or break off the excess tip. Work two to four turns of thread forward through the hackle to the hook eye. Wax an inch of thread, make a four-turn whip finish, and clip the thread. Don't cement the head when tying Gossamer silk, as it kills the color.

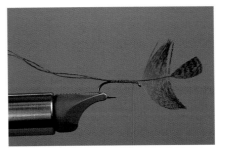

METHOD 2

Step 1. Use this method, which uses floss and has no thorax, if you cannot find Pearsall's Gossamer silk or prefer the traditional tie without a fur thorax. Start orange 6/0 thread just behind the eye. Strip fuzzy fibers from the stem of a feather, and flare the remaining fibers at 90-degree angles. Tie in the feather with the concave side toward you. Separate four-strand orange floss into two-strand sections. Tie in the floss, and take thread wraps over it to a point just past the hook point.

Step 2. Wind floss forward in a single layer to the hackle tie-in point. Tie it off there and clip the excess. The body should be slender and without taper. Take two turns of hackle, one behind the hook eye and the second behind the first. Capture the hackle tip with two thread turns, break or cut the excess tip, and work a few thread turns through the hackle to the hook eye. Whip-finish the fly and clip the thread. Cement the head when using 6/0 thread.

Useful Variations

The Grouse & Orange, Partridge & Yellow, and Partridge & Green cover the colors of many mayfly duns, caddisfly pupae, and stonefly adults. They are the basic soft-hackles that you should tie and carry, if you carry no others. They are useful whenever you're exploring new water, especially if it's shallow and riffled and you want to cover it quickly to see where trout might be found.

The March Brown Spider is specific for march brown mayfly hatches and an infinity of caddis species with brown wings and tan bodies. It's effective just after a hatch of the mayfly duns, when trout turn from floating duns to taking drowned cripples. It often works better than a dry fly when brownish caddis adults are on the wing.

The Red Hackle works well when olive-bodied caddis are in the air and on the water. The Starling & Herl is usually better than a matching dry fly when small, dark American grannom caddisflies (Brachycentridae) are hatching. The Snipe

& Yellow works when any of a myriad of tiny, light-colored caddis are out and about.

| 1 | 2 | 3 |
| 4 | 5 | 6 |

1	Partridge & Yellow		2	Partridge & Green		3	March Brown Spider
	SYLVESTER NEMES			SYLVESTER NEMES			SYLVESTER NEMES
Hook	Standard wet fly, sizes 10, **12, 14,** 16		Hook	Standard wet fly, sizes 10, **12, 14,** 16		Hook	Standard wet fly, sizes 10, **12, 14,** 16
Thread	Yellow Gossamer silk or 6/0		Thread	Green Gossamer silk or 6/0		Thread	Orange Gossamer silk or 6/0
Hackle	Gray partridge		Hackle	Brown partridge		Hackle	Brown partridge
Body	Working silk or yellow floss		Body	Working silk or green floss		Rib	Oval gold tinsel
Thorax	Hare's mask fur		Thorax	Hare's mask fur		Body	Hare's mask fur

4	Red Hackle		5	Starling & Herl		6	Snipe & Yellow
	JAMES LEISENRING		Hook	Standard wet fly, sizes 14, **16, 18,** 20		Hook	Standard wet fly, sizes 14, **16, 18,** 20
Hook	Standard wet fly, sizes 12, **14, 16,** 18		Thread	Black 6/0 or 8/0		Thread	Yellow Gossamer silk or 6/0
Thread	Red Gossamer silk or 6/0		Hackle	Starling back feather		Hackle	Snipe wing shoulder feather
Hackle	Brown or furnace hen		Body	Peacock herl		Body	Working silk or yellow floss
Body	Bronze peacock herl						

Fishing Notes

Originally, two or three soft-hackled wets were used on the same leader. They were fished upstream in riffles, runs, and pools of small, fast waters. I still use them this way on my tiny home streams and have had success fishing them this way all over the world. Whenever the sun is bright and small-stream trout splash at your dry flies but refuse to take them, switch to a soft-hackle, or a pair of them. Creep close, shorten the cast, and fish them upstream just like drys. Watch the line tip or leader for any twitch or dart, the water for a wink of light. If you see anything suspicious, raise the rod to set the hook.

It's more common to fish soft-hackles on larger streams and rivers, with casts quartering across broad riffles and runs. Let the fly, or pair of flies, swing down and around. Slow the swing with mends if the fly or pair of flies moves faster than a natural insect might swim in the same water. Take a step or two between casts, and repeat the cast to let the flies explore all the water as you work downstream.

You won't have any trouble noticing takes. Respond gently when you feel a tap or a tug so that you don't set the hook too hard and break your tippet.

Sylvester Nemes, author of The Soft-Hackled Fly, *playing a trout in a classic soft-hackle riffle on the Yellowstone River.*

WINGLESS WET FLIES: FLYMPHS

The late Pete Hidy, coauthor of *The Art of Tying the Wet Fly* (with James Leisenring, Dodd, Mead & Co., 1941), coined the term *flymph* for wingless wet flies. They represent insects that are not yet *flies* but no longer *nymphs*—hence *flymphs*.

A flymph can represent a mayfly or small stonefly nymph in the transitional stage near the surface. It can also represent a mayfly dun or stonefly adult that has drowned, a caddis pupa on its way to the surface, or a caddis adult swimming down to the bottom to lay its eggs. Trout feast during all of these activities. Flymphs fool them.

The March Brown Flymph, originated by angling entomologist Rick Hafele, fishes for both the emerging nymph and the drowned dun of the march brown mayfly. It's an important example of the flymph phenomenon. You tie on a wingless wet fly that's the color and size of whatever adult insect is visible in the air or on the water and fish it just beneath the surface to feeding trout. It often works better than a dry fly tied to match the same insect.

March Brown Flymph

RICK HAFELE

Hook	Standard wet fly, sizes 10, **12**, **14**, 16
Thread	Red Pearsall's Gossamer silk or 6/0
Hackle	Furnace or brown hen
Tails	Furnace or brown hen or rooster
Body	Hare's mask fur

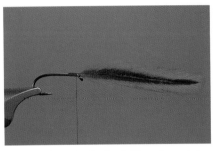

Step 1. Wax an inch of red silk, and start it just behind the hook eye. Clip the excess tag. The thread is the undercolor desired for this fly. If you can't find Gossamer silk, use red 6/0 thread, but you won't get the full undercolor benefit from the thread because it's so much finer. Select a hen neck feather with fibers two hook gaps long. Strip fuzzy fibers from the base of the stem, and tie in the feather with the concave side toward you and the hackle tip extending over the hook eye.

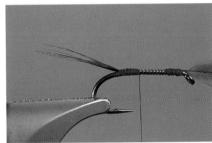

Step 2. Wrap the working thread to the bend of the hook. Select eight to twelve hackle fibers from the same neck from which you took the hackle. If no fibers are long enough, which is common with a grade 1 or 2 hen neck, use brown rooster hackle fibers for the tail. Measure the tail fibers the length of the hook, and tie them in at the bend of the hook. I prefer my flymph tails to be cocked slightly upward, for a rakish look. To accomplish this, take a couple turns of thread tight under the base of the tails.

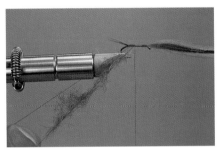

Step 3. The body of a flymph should be loose and spiky. By tying with a dubbing loop, you double the red thread and increase the desired undercolor. Begin by waxing several inches of thread with sticky dubbing wax. Spread the dubbing fur, with guard hairs mixed in, on the thread. Just touch it to the wax so that it remains in place, rather than twisting it onto the thread as you normally do with dubbing. Catch the thread over the forefinger of your off hand, and return it to the shank to form a dubbing loop.

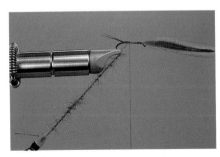

Step 4. Coax the thread loop off your forefinger, and let it collapse onto the fur, being sure the fur is captured between the thread strands. Twirl the tip of the thread between your fingers until the thread and fur are twisted into a tight but spiky dubbing rope. This should be slightly tapered, fatter at the far end, resulting in a tapered body when you wind it. Attach your hackle pliers to the end of the twisted rope to make it easier to wrap the body.

Step 5. Wind the body forward from the base of the tail to the hackle tie-in point. If necessary, use the thumb and fingertips of your off hand to hold the previous fur wraps back while you abut the next wraps directly in front of them. The goal is a thick but loose body, with lots of fibers sticking out to move in the current. You can tidy up the body, but it should remain shaggy. Remove only those stray dubbing fibers that will be longer than the hackle after it is wound.

Step 6. Take the thread to a point about one-third to one-half the shank length behind the hackle. Take one turn of hackle just behind the hook eye, a second turn tucked behind the first, the next halfway to the thread, and a final turn of hackle at the thread. Capture the hackle stem with a couple turns of thread, and clip or break off the excess tip. Return the working thread to the hook eye, working several turns forward through the hackle to lock it in. Make a neat thread head with just a few wraps of silk, whip-finish, and clip the thread.

Useful Variations

Useful variations of the flymph style cover the color spectrum of natural insects. Think in terms of the few common color themes repeated by mayflies, stoneflies, and caddis.

The March Brown Flymph and Hare's Ear Flymph fish for dark brown and light brown naturals of all the major insect types. The Ginger Wingless and Pale Watery Wingless fish for pale caddis, sulfur mayflies, and yellow sally stoneflies. The Blue Dun Wingless and Little Olive Flymph fish for the many mayflies, stoneflies, and caddis with gray or olive bodies. The Little Dark Flymph is tied for heavy hatches of the nearly black American grannoms that emerge in early spring and then again in fall, on streams all across our continent and on several others.

I recommend that you choose at least a dark and a light flymph to cover the broadest range of naturals with the narrowest range of flies. Choose either the March Brown Flymph or Hare's Ear Flymph for the dark fly, and the Ginger Wingless or Pale Watery Wingless for the light. Tie other variations when you encounter insects that they match and trout are feeding on them beneath the surface rather than on top.

1	2	3
4	5	6

1	Hare's Ear Flymph
Hook	Standard wet fly, sizes 10, **12, 14**, 16
Thread	Red Gossamer silk or 6/0
Hackle	Brown or furnace hen
Rib	Oval gold tinsel
Tails	Brown or furnace hen or rooster
Body	Light hare's mask fur

2	Ginger Wingless
Hook	Standard wet fly, sizes 12, **14, 16**, 18
Thread	Yellow Gossamer silk or 6/0
Hackle	Dark ginger hen
Rib	Oval gold tinsel
Tails	Dark ginger hen or rooster
Body	Golden-brown fur dubbing

3	Pale Watery Wingless
	JAMES LEISENRING
Hook	Standard wet fly, sizes 12, **14, 16**, 18
Thread	Yellow Gossamer silk or 6/0
Hackle	Light ginger hen
Rib	Oval gold tinsel
Tails	Light ginger hen or rooster
Body	Creamy olive fur dubbing

4	Blue Dun Wingless
	JAMES LEISENRING
Hook	Standard wet fly, sizes 12, **14, 16**, 18
Thread	Yellow Gossamer silk or 6/0
Hackle	Blue dun hen
Rib	Oval silver tinsel
Tails	Blue dun hen or rooster
Body	Muskrat belly fur

5	Little Olive Flymph
	DAVE HUGHES
Hook	Standard wet fly, sizes 14, **16, 18**, 20
Thread	Green Gossamer silk or 6/0
Hackle	Blue dun hen
Rib	Oval gold tinsel
Tails	Blue dun hen or rooster
Body	Olive fur dubbing

6	Little Dark Flymph
	DAVE HUGHES
Hook	Standard wet fly, sizes 14, **16, 18**, 20
Thread	Black 6/0 or 8/0
Hackle	Dark blue dun or black hen
Tails	Dark blue dun or black hen
Body	Peacock herl

Fishing Notes

I fish flymphs most often when an adult insect is abundant, trout are active and seem to be feeding on what I'm seeing, and I've tried dry flies but they didn't work. The natural is most often an adult caddis. The trout are usually feeding on pupae or swimming adults so close to the surface that the visible rises appear to be on top. But more caddis are taken beneath the surface than on it. Whenever I see caddis in the air but don't do well with drys, I switch to a flymph or another style of wet fly in the size and color of the natural in the air. It usually solves the problem.

If trout are scattered, fish flymphs with the traditional wet-fly swing. Cast across the current, and let the fly swing down and around. It's often wise to cast two flies, one light and one dark, to see which the trout prefer.

If trout are feeding in fixed stations, try to collect a natural, and select a wet dressing the same size and color. Work on a specific rising trout. Take a position upstream and off to one side. Cast down and across, just above and beyond the fish. Give the fly a tug to pop it through the surface film. Then let it drift and swing in front of the trout. A take to the wet will usually be just as visible as a rise to a dry.

In such heavily fished water as the Firehole River in Yellowstone Park, flymphs can be deadly if fished at the right times.

TRADITIONAL WINGED WET FLIES

Winged wet flies were out of use for some years but have been rediscovered because they catch so many trout and because they're so easy and so much fun to fish.

These traditional wet flies resemble many natural insects. Mayfly duns drown during a hatch, and trout feed on them in the hour or so after the hatch. Females of the two most abundant trout-stream caddis groups, gray and spotted sedges, swim to the bottom to deposit their eggs. Egg-depositing stoneflies drown and are taken beneath the surface almost as often as on top. All of this feeding is less visible than when trout are taking floating adults, so it's harder to notice when it happens.

A winged wet fly in the correct size and color is the perfect match when trout are taking these insects subsurface. It's no accident that wet flies worked so well in fly-fishing history and that they still work as well today.

The listed Leadwing Coachman is an excellent searching wet fly. It's also the imitation of choice when gray sedges lay their eggs over bright riffles but dry flies fail to coax trout feeding on them.

Leadwing Coachman	
Hook	Standard wet fly, sizes 10, **12, 14**, 16
Thread	Black 6/0 or 8/0
Hackle	Furnace or brown hen
Rib	Oval silver tinsel
Body	Peacock herl
Wing	Gray mallard primary feather section

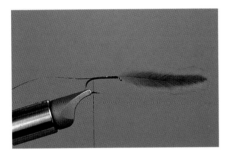

Step 1. Start the thread behind the hook eye. Select a hen hackle feather with fibers one and a half to two hook gaps long, or the length of the hook shank. Strip fuzzy fibers from the lower end of the stem, and tie in the feather with the concave side facing you, the tip of the feather extending over the hook eye. Clip 3 to 5 inches of ribbing tinsel from the spool. Tie it in where you clip the excess hackle stem, and layer thread over it to the bend of the hook.

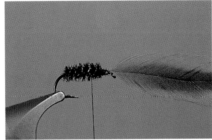

Step 2. Select two or three peacock herls from an eyed feather. Peel them from the stem rather than cut them; the pigtail ends will make it easier to twirl them with the thread. Tie in the herls by their tips at the bend of the hook; make the last turns at the back soft. Form a thread loop, twist the herl and thread loop together, and wind the herl forward to a point about one hook-eye length behind the eye. Tie off the herl, clip the excess, and take your thread back over the body about one-third the shank length.

Step 3. Wind the hackle over the front third of the body. This is more like a drowned insect than the normal tie, with all of the hackle at the head. Capture the hackle tip with two turns of thread, and either twitch the hackle to break it off against the thread or clip the excess. Work thread wraps through the hackle to the hook eye. Use sparse turns of thread to lay an even, tapered base for the wings. End with your thread at the back of the head. The first turn of thread over the wings must be the farthest back.

Step 4. Select matching primary or secondary feathers from paired mallard wings. Clip a section about the width of the hook gap from the upper, darker half of each feather. Marry these sections together carefully, with their concave sides facing each other. Hold the married sections with their longest edge up, and measure them just past the end of the hook. This sample dressing has no tail, but the general rule on wet-fly wing length is to the midpoint of the tail.

Step 5. In a well-tied wet fly, the wing is centered over the shank, upright, not canted or twisted. A cocked wet-fly wing becomes a rudder that causes the fly to corkscrew in the current. Hold the paired sections behind the hook eye in a tight pinch with your off hand. Lay a single soft loop over the sections, at the back of what will become the head. If this first turn is not the farthest back, subsequent turns will roll the wing out of position after you've taken the trouble to set it correctly.

Step 6. Hold the wing firmly in place, and draw the soft loop down onto it. Pull the bobbin tip straight down, or even toward you, under the hook shank. This compresses the stacked wing fibers directly onto the top of the hook. This can be learned and practiced as a slow movement, but a quick *pop* that seats the soft loop firmly and abruptly places the wing best. Secure the wing with five to ten thread wraps forward from the first. Clip the excess wing butts. Form a neat thread head, whip-finish, clip the thread, and cement the head.

Useful Variations

The most useful variations on the winged wet-fly style cover the color spectrum of natural trout food forms. The Leadwing Coachman and Hare's Ear Wet fish specifically for the two most important groups of trout stream caddis: the gray and spotted sedges. Light and Dark Cahills, plus the Blue-Winged Olive, are useful during many mayfly hatches. An appropriate wet fly will commonly outfish a dry fly in the presence of small stoneflies: the yellow sallies, olive sallies, and little brown stones.

The Alder is specific for prolific June and July alderfly hatches on most lakes and ponds, as well as some streams. It's a fly I would never be without, because I like fishing lakes. The Royal Coachman, with its bright wing, is an attractor that is listed because it catches lots of trout.

Again, I recommend selecting at least one light and one dark dressing for your basic fly boxes. That might mean the Royal Coachman and Leadwing Coachman. Light and Dark Cahills also make an excellent complementary pair. I fish the

Light Cahill and Alder more than other traditional winged wets. But I tie and fish wet flies far more than the average angler, and consider all of the listed dressings essential.

1	2	3
4	5	6

1	Hare's Ear Wet
Hook	Standard wet fly, sizes 10, **12, 14,** 16
Thread	Orange 6/0 or 8/0
Tails	Pheasant tail fibers
Rib	Oval gold tinsel
Body	Hare's mask fur
Wing	Partridge primary or secondary wing feather sections

2	Light Cahill
Hook	Standard wet fly, sizes **12, 14,** 16, 18
Thread	Tan 6/0 or 8/0
Hackle	Ginger hen
Tails	Ginger hen or rooster
Body	Cream fur dubbing
Wing	Wood duck flank fibers

3	Dark Cahill
Hook	Standard wet fly, sizes **12, 14,** 16, 18
Thread	Black 6/0 or 8/0
Hackle	Furnace or brown hen
Tails	Furnace or brown hen or rooster
Body	Muskrat back fur
Wing	Wood duck flank fibers

4	Blue-Winged Olive
Hook	Standard wet fly, sizes 12, **14, 16,** 18
Thread	Gray 6/0 or 8/0
Hackle	Blue dun hen
Tails	Blue dun hen or rooster
Rib	Oval gold tinsel
Body	Olive fur dubbing
Wing	Mallard wing feather sections

5	Alder
Hook	Standard wet fly, sizes 8, **10, 12,** 14
Thread	Black 6/0 or 8/0
Hackle	Furnace or black hen
Body	Peacock herl
Wing	Mottled turkey or grouse wing feather sections

6	Royal Coachman
Hook	Standard wet fly, sizes 10, **12, 14,** 16
Thread	Black 6/0 or 8/0
Hackle	Dark brown hen
Tails	Golden pheasant tippets
Body	Peacock herl, red floss, peacock herl
Wing	White mallard wing feather sections

Fishing Notes

A wet fly is often the best device with which to explore a stream, discover where the trout are holding, and see what fly they might be willing to take. It often helps to try two on the same leader, one light and one dark or one small and one large. Always offer the trout two very different flies, never two alike. The object is not to catch two fish on one cast, but to discover which one they'll accept consistently.

One of the best ways to cover water and find fish, to this day, is to tie a wet fly to your tippet, drop another off the tag end of the tippet knot, then cast and step, cast and step, working your way downstream, covering all of the water. Cast quartering across and down. Let your flies nose in and out of all the water. Cause them to linger around visible obstructions to the current such as boulders or logs. Make sure they swing across any current seam between fast water and slow. Show them to every bit of potential holding water. Let them find the trout for you.

If the current is slow, you might find it necessary to toss a downstream mend into the line to speed the drift and swing of

Traditional wet flies are far from out of fashion in the eyes of trout, especially when they're fished on the swing through a riffle or run just at dusk.

the flies. More often, the current will be fast enough that you'll increase your chances by using upstream mends to slow them to the speed a natural insect might travel.

SPARKLE CADDIS PUPAE

Gary LaFontaine, from Deer Lodge, Montana, has applied more science to fly fishing than has any other writer. He observes aquatic insects in their own environment by diving down to watch them. When he experiments with flies, he has friends fish them while he goes below to observe the way trout react to them. Gary's book *Caddisflies* (Winchester Press, 1981) is a fine condensation of his research and experience.

Gary found that caddis pupae rise to the surface encased in a bubble of air. He then tracked down the right material—Sparkle Yarn, under the label Antron yarn—to imitate this bubble beneath the water. The result is his series of Sparkle Pupae. Deep Sparkle Pupae represent the insects adrift on the bottom. Emergent Sparkle Pupae represent them as they near the surface. Diving Caddis represent adults diving down to the bottom to lay their eggs. The key factor in each is the sparkle from the yarn.

Gary ties each style in eleven colors. The patterns listed here represent the most common colors of caddis for consideration as additions to your list of essential flies.

Green Deep Sparkle Pupa

GARY LAFONTAINE

Hook	Standard wet fly, sizes 12, **14, 16,** 18
Weight	Underweight or normal
Thread	Brown 6/0 or 8/0
Overbody	Medium green Antron yarn
Underbody	One-third olive Antron yarn, two-thirds bright green fur or synthetic
Hackle	Grouse fibers
Head	Brown fur dubbing

Step 1. Gary LaFontaine weights the Deep Sparkle Pupa with around fifteen turns of lead wire the diameter of the hook shank. I underweight mine, using lead wire one size finer, and add split shot to the leader to get them down when desired. Start the thread, lock the weight in, and wrap the thread to the hook bend. Use a fine-toothed comb or your bodkin point to tease out a skein of Antron Sparkle Yarn. It should be about twice the length of the hook.

Step 2. Split the teased yarn in half. Tie half on top of the shank, at the bend of the hook. Tie the other half on the underside of the hook. If you have a rotary vise, reverse it for this operation. If not, pop the yarn in place with a soft loop from beneath. You can also tie in all of the yarn with a soft loop and a couple turns of thread, then tug it to separate it into top and bottom portions before securing it with more thread wraps. Clip the excess.

Step 3. From an Antron yarn skein, snip one part into ⅛- to ¼-inch bits. Add two parts of bright green fur, Antron dubbing, or another synthetic. Blend them together in a blender or coffee grinder until they're mixed well. Dub an underbody of this mixture to a point about one-fourth the length of the shank behind the eye. The body should be somewhat portly; caddis pupae are fat.

Step 4. Bring the top part of the teased-out overbody yarn forward to the end of the body, and tie it off. Be sure it's loose and rides above the body. The purpose is to enclose the body, not to draw a tight shellback over it. Bring the bottom part of the overbody yarn forward, and tie it off at the end of the body. Again, it should be loose. Clip the excess.

Step 5. Select three to four fibers from a grouse wing secondary feather, and measure them just a bit longer than the hook. Tie them in on the near side of the fly, so that they sweep back along the upper part of the body. Repeat the process on the far side. Clip the excess butts. These fibers represent the antennae and legs of the natural caddis pupa.

Step 6. Dub a short, fat head of brown fur. Form a neat thread head, whip-finish, clip the thread, and cement the head. Use your bodkin point to spread the teased yarn overbody around the underbody. Insert the bodkin between the overbody and the underbody, and draw the overbody back so it ends at about the end of the hook or even slightly behind it. The finished fly should have the body encased in yarn, just as a natural rises to the surface with its body encased in a bubble of air.

Useful Variations

The Green Deep Sparkle Pupa imitates the pupae of most gray sedges and many spotted sedges. It belongs in your basic box. The Yellow Deep Sparkle Pupa and the Ginger Sparkle Deep Pupa imitate many tan to brown species.

Green, Yellow, and Ginger Emergent Sparkle pupae represent the same groups near the top rather than the bottom. The Green Diving Caddis is the correct color for the olive-bodied gray sedges. You would be wise to tie the same fly style in yellow and ginger variations if you find that the green one works well for you and you'd like to try others.

The entire range of eleven colors that Gary LaFontaine lists, for all three styles—Deep, Emergent, and Diving—should be investigated if you fish over insect hatches. When you encounter a hatch of caddis that is hard to solve, chances are good that a solution lies somewhere within the list of flies that Gary gives in his masterful *Caddisflies*.

1	**2**	**3**
4	**5**	**6**

1	*Yellow Deep Sparkle Pupa*
	GARY LAFONTAINE
Hook	Standard wet fly, sizes 12, **14, 16,** 18
Weight	Underweight or normal
Thread	Brown 6/0 or 8/0
Overbody	Gold Antron yarn
Underbody	1/2 gold Antron yarn, 1/2 brown fur or synthetic, mixed
Hackle	Wood duck flank fibers
Head	Brown fur dubbing

2	*Ginger Deep Sparkle Pupa*
	GARY LAFONTAINE
Hook	Standard wet fly, sizes 12, **14, 16,** 18
Weight	Underweight or normal
Thread	Tan 6/0 or 8/0
Overbody	Amber Antron yarn
Underbody	1/2 amber Antron yarn, 1/2 cream fur or synthetic, mixed
Hackle	Wood duck flank fibers
Head	Cream fur dubbing

3	*Green Emergent Sparkle Pupa*
	GARY LAFONTAINE
Hook	Standard wet fly, sizes 12, **14, 16,** 18
Thread	Brown 6/0 or 8/0
Overbody	Medium green Antron yarn
Underbody	1/3 olive Antron yarn, 2/3 bright green fur or synthetic, mixed
Wing	Dark brown deer body hair
Head	Brown marabou herl

4	*Yellow Emergent Sparkle Pupa*
	GARY LAFONTAINE
Hook	Standard wet fly, sizes 12, **14, 16,** 18
Thread	Brown 6/0 or 8/0
Overbody	Gold Antron yarn
Underbody	1/2 gold Antron yarn, 1/2 brown fur or synthetic, mixed
Wing	Light brown deer body hair
Head	Brown marabou herl

5	*Ginger Emergent Sparkle Pupa*
	GARY LAFONTAINE
Hook	Standard wet fly, sizes 12, **14, 16,** 18
Thread	Tan 6/0 or 8/0
Overbody	Amber Antron yarn
Underbody	1/2 amber Antron yarn, 1/2 cream fur or synthetic, mixed
Wing	Light brown deer body hair
Head	Cream marabou herl

6	*Green Diving Caddis*
	GARY LAFONTAINE
Hook	Standard wet fly, sizes 12, **14, 16,** 18
Thread	Brown 6/0 or 8/0
Body	Green Antron dubbing
Underwing	Dark brown grouse fibers
Overwing	Clear Antron yarn
Hackle	Brown rooster, short and sparse

Fishing Notes

The Deep Sparkle Pupa style is designed to be fished on the bottom, dead drift. Gary LaFontaine recommends getting it down with a wet-tip line. I often use the shot and indicator method to deliver all nymphs to the bottom and to show them over all potential lies.

I fish flies in the Deep Sparkle Pupa style on the traditional wet-fly swing, in water that's moving briskly, when I notice trout working actively but they refuse dry flies. I want these wets to fish just inches deep. It's often the solution to catching selective rising trout that refuse a dry fly when caddis adults are in the air.

Emergent Sparkle Pupae and Diving Caddis styles are both designed to be fished near the surface. If you're working over a specific feeding trout, move into position downstream and cast upstream to it, just as if you were using a dry fly. If you're fishing over scattered trout that are actively feeding, try swinging either style of fly through them slowly.

Gary LaFontaine's Sparkle Pupa patterns can turn your luck quickly when the normal run of dry flies and nymphs fail.

MUDDLER MINNOWS

Today the Muddler, made famous by Dan Bailey, is considered a western fly, used to extract big trout from big water. It was originated by Don Gapen for smallmouth bass and brook trout in rivers flowing into the Great Lakes. A sculpin and mad-tom imitation, it works well in any waters with populations of bottom-hugging bullhead-shaped baitfish, which means almost everywhere that trout swim.

The Muddler can be tied weighted to fish the bottom. It can be tied unweighted but with an oval tinsel body, which will deliver it to the mid-depths if the right line is used. It can be tied as a dry fly and fished as a grasshopper or large stonefly imitation. The Muddler is mandatory in any exploratory-fly box.

Though best known for the portly browns and rainbows it extracts in its largest sizes, 2, 4, and 6, I recommend you tie it and fish it more often in sizes 8, 10, and even 12. These smaller sizes are more useful for most trout fishing and easier to cast with the 4-, 5-, and 6-weight outfits most of us now fish most of the time.

Muddler Minnow

DON GAPEN

Hook	3X or 4X long, sizes 2, 4, 6, **8, 10, 12**
Thread	Yellow 3/0 or 6/0
Tail	Mottled turkey tail feather sections
Body	Oval or flat gold tinsel
Underwing	Fox squirrel tail
Overwing	Mottled turkey tail feather sections
Collar	Tips of head hair
Head	Deer body hair, spun and clipped

Step 1. Start the thread one-third the shank length behind the eye, and layer it to the bend. Clip two turkey tail sections from paired feathers, marry them, measure them half the hook length, and tie them in with a soft loop just as you would a wet-fly wing, at the bend of the hook. Layer thread over the tail butts two-thirds of the shank length before clipping the excess. Tie in oval or flat tinsel at that point, and secure it back to the bend. Wrap the tinsel body forward over two-thirds of the shank, tie it off, and clip the excess.

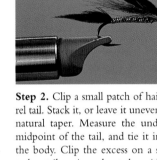

Step 2. Clip a small patch of hair from a squirrel tail. Stack it, or leave it uneven so it ends in a natural taper. Measure the underwing to the midpoint of the tail, and tie it in at the end of the body. Clip the excess on a slant. Clip two turkey tail sections about the width of the hook gap. Marry them, and measure the wing to the midpoint of the tail. Tie in the wing with a soft loop and several turns of thread forward over the squirrel tail butts. Clip the excess. Leave the hook shank bare in front of the wing tie-in point.

Step 3. Select a small clump from a patch of hollow deer hair. Clip the hair from the hide, remove all fuzz from the butts, and align the tips in your stacker. Measure the hair slightly longer than the full length of the hook, and clip the butts straight across to even them. Move the hair so the tips reach just to the back end of the body. Hold the hair in place over the wing tie-in point, and work the hair around the hook shank. Take two soft loops around the hair without pulling them tight and without releasing the hair.

Step 4. Draw the soft loops tight and let go of the hair at the same time. The hollow hair will flare around the thread, causing the collar to spread out around the body and wings. You might have to coax it into the full circle. The shorter hair butts will flare and become part of the spun and clipped hair head. Take several more tight turns of thread forward through the hair butts, until the thread reaches bare shank. This first spun hair should be sparse, with just enough for the collar surrounding the wings.

Step 5. Take a few turns of thread around the bare hook shank in front of the deer-hair butts. Use the nails of your tying-hand thumb and forefinger to pack the hair butts back against the wing tie-in point. At the same time, push the few thread wraps in front of the hair butts back against the hair. This forms a block, or dam, to stand the hair up at 90-degree angles to the hook shank. It also makes room for a second, larger clump of spun hair on the bare shank behind the hook eye.

Step 6. Clip a larger clump of deer hair, clean all fuzz from the butts, and clip straight across the butts and tips to form a bundle 1/2 inch long. Hold this in place over the bare shank, take two soft loops around it, then draw the loops tight and let the hair go at the same time. It will roll around the hook and flare. Take several more turns of thread forward through the hair to the hook eye. Hold the hair back and whip-finish the head. Clip the thread. Give the fly a neat and tapered haircut, straight across the bottom, slightly tapered on the sides and top.

Useful Variations

The standard Muddler Minnow is tied with oval tinsel, which adds some weight. It doesn't sink quickly, but it does get far enough down that it doesn't send a wake up to the surface. If you fish often in fast water, or on large rivers where a deep swing will show your fly to more trout, consider weighting some of your Muddlers.

The most useful variation is the Muddler Dry, tied so it floats. It can be cast to banks and drifted along them as a large stonefly or hopper. If trout ignore it, you can tug it under and retrieve it for a few feet before lifting it for the next cast.

The Marabou Muddler series is next in importance. Members of my home club, the Rainland Flycasters in Astoria, Oregon, call the Black Marabou Muddler the Black & Ugly and use it so extensively that no one dares leave home without it. I recommend adding the Black Marabou Muddler and the standard Muddler Minnow to your essential list of trout flies, and tie others if you find you need them.

| 1 | 2 | 3 |
| 4 | 5 | 6 |

1	Muddler Dry
Hook	3X or 4X long, sizes 6, 8, **10, 12**
Thread	Yellow 3/0 or 6/0
Tail	Mottled turkey feather sections
Body	Yellow yarn or fur
Underwing	White calf tail
Overwing	Mottled turkey feather sections
Collar and head	Deer body hair

2	Black Marabou Muddler
Hook	3X or 4X long, sizes 4, 6, **8, 10,** 12
Weight	20 to 30 turns of lead wire
Thread	Black 3/0 or 6/0
Tail	Black marabou
Body	Black fur or synthetic dubbing
Wing	Black marabou
Collar and head	Black dyed deer hair

3	White Marabou Muddler
Hook	3X or 4X long, sizes 4, 6, **8, 10,** 12
Weight	20 to 30 turns of lead wire
Thread	White 3/0 or 6/0
Tail	White marabou
Body	White fur or synthetic dubbing
Wing	White marabou
Collar and head	Natural deer hair

4	Yellow Marabou Muddler
Hook	3X or 4X long, sizes 4, 6, **8, 10,** 12
Weight	20 to 30 turns of lead wire
Thread	Yellow 3/0 or 6/0
Tail	Yellow marabou
Body	Yellow fur or synthetic dubbing
Wing	Yellow marabou
Collar and head	Natural deer hair

5	Olive Marabou Muddler
Hook	3X or 4X long, sizes 4, 6, **8, 10,** 12
Weight	20 to 30 turns of lead wire
Thread	Olive 3/0 or 6/0
Tail	Olive marabou
Body	Olive fur or synthetic dubbing
Wing	Olive marabou
Collar and head	Natural deer hair

6	Spuddler
	DAN BAILEY AND RED MONICAL
Hook	3X or 4X long, sizes 2, 4, **6, 8,** 10
Thread	Brown 3/0 or 6/0
Tail	Fox squirrel tail
Body	Cream fur dubbing
Underwing	Fox squirrel tail
Overwing	Silver or honey badger hackles
Collar and head	Antelope or deer body hair

Fishing Notes

The Muddler Minnow can be escorted to the bottom in medium streams to big rivers with a sinking-tip, wet-head, or full-sinking line. It should be allowed to tumble along there or given an occasional twitch of the rod tip to make it look as if it's crippled and trying to right itself and swim. I often fish Muddlers over riffles and shallow runs on a wet-fly swing, just a foot or so down. The standard tie, unweighted but tied with oval tinsel, is perfect for this. You can use a floating or sinking-tip line. This method works best at dawn and dusk, when big trout are on the prowl.

The Muddler Dry should be fished near the banks, combining a few feet of dead drift followed by a short retrieve. The flies in the Marabou Muddler series are all weighted and designed to be fished near the bottom or the banks. They are also deadly in lakes and ponds, and on smallmouth and largemouth bass as well. The Black Marabou Muddler is especially effective in waters with populations of leeches.

Explore broad riffles and runs for large trout with a Muddler Minnow or variation.

HAIRWING AND FEATHERWING STREAMERS

The golden age of streamers lasted two or three decades, ending in the 1960s. But these beautiful flies represent things that trout still eat, and they still catch trout. If you'd like to be armed to fish the full array of trout tactics, in order to take fish in all sorts of conditions, a few of these traditional dressings should be kept ready in your basic fly boxes. When you find big trout pursuing baitfish, you can coax them to these minnowlike imitations and to little else.

Traditional streamers also make excellent searching patterns. In early spring, when the water is still high, unclear, and cold, then again in fall, when the water is low and clear but cooling, trout are interested in feeding but don't find much available in the way of natural insects. A streamer fished slow and near the bottom will entice them into a take if you place it where they can see it.

Streamers are usually thought of as big flies, sizes 4 and 6, but I recommend that you tie them in sizes 8 and 10. You might be surprised at the results these smaller streamers bring.

Mickey Finn

Hook	6X long, sizes 6, **8, 10**, 12
Thread	Black 3/0 or 6/0
Rib	Fine oval silver tinsel
Body	Flat silver tinsel
Underwing	Yellow bucktail
Midwing	Red bucktail
Overwing	Yellow bucktail

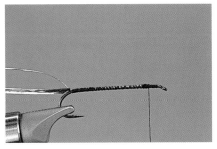

MICKEY FINN

Step 1. Start your thread just behind the hook eye. Cut several inches of body and ribbing tinsels; don't short yourself. Capture them together under the thread just behind the eye, and secure them back to the hook bend. If you use mylar tinsel for the body, with one side silver and the other gold, tie it in with the silver side against the hook shank. Return the thread in a few turns to a point about two hook-eye lengths behind the eye.

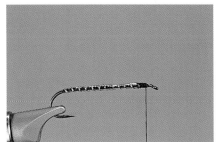

Step 2. Wind the body forward. If it is mylar, it will reverse itself, and the silver side will show. Tie it off at a point about two hook-eye lengths behind the eye. Be sure to leave room for tying in the wing and for a substantial head. The body tinsel turns should be slightly overlapped to form an even body. Wide tinsel is easier to work with than narrow, but the best size of tinsel depends on the size of fly you're tying. Counterwind the ribbing tinsel over the body tinsel in eight to twelve evenly spaced turns.

Step 3. Clip a small patch of yellow bucktail from the hide. Align the tips in your stacker. Measure the hair just past the end of the hook; if the fly had a tail, the wing would reach to the end of it. Hold this hair firmly in place at the end of the body, and tie it in with a single layer of thread wraps forward halfway to the hook eye. Clip the butts on a slant. Clip an equal amount of red bucktail, align the tips, measure it to the same point, and tie it in over the yellow. Clip the butts on the same slant.

Step 4. Clip a patch of yellow bucktail equal in amount to the underwing and midwing together. Align the tips, measure the hair to the end of the underwing and midwing, and tie it in over the previous hair butts. Trim the butts on a slant down to the hook eye. Layer an even thread head from the hook eye to the base of the wing. Whip-finish once or twice, clip the thread, and cement the head. The sheen of cement is traditional on a streamer. After the first coat has penetrated the thread wraps, apply a second.

LIGHT SPRUCE

Step 1. Layer the hook with thread. Select four or five peacock sword fibers, measure them one-third the shank length, and tie them in at the bend. Capture red floss along with them, and wind both to the midpoint of the hook. Clip the excess, wind the floss body forward to mid-shank, and tie it off. Tie in three to five peacock herl fibers, twist them with the thread, and wind to about two hook-eye lengths behind the eye.

Step 2. Prepare a hackle with fibers two hook gaps long, and tie it in with the concave side toward the shank, so the fibers will sweep back when wound. Wind four to five turns of hackle, tie it off, and clip the excess tip. Select two matched feathers from the same neck, pair them back-to-back, measure them to the end of the tail, and strip all fibers below the tie-in point. Tie them in at the head of the fly. Reverse the stems and capture them under a second layer of thread to lock them in. Clip the excess stems. Whip-finish and apply cement.

Useful Variations

You probably don't want to overload your fly boxes with streamers. You should, however, select one bright and one dark pattern, tying and carrying each in a narrow range of sizes. If your luck on them warrants it, tie and carry more. I recommend the Mickey Finn or Royal Coachman Bucktail as the bright searching streamer and the Dark Spruce as the drab fly for fishing when trout seem bashful about taking the bright one. You get a feel for this in your fishing, and it doesn't take long. The best hint to use a bright fly is a dark day, and for a dark fly, a bright day. A switch to a smaller and darker streamer is always wise when even a single trout comes at your fly but turns away without taking it.

If you continually notice trout fry darting around your feet in the shallows, try the Little Rainbow Trout or Little Brook Trout, depending on the predominant species of fish caught in the waters where you're wading. If your waters contain dace, tie and carry the famous Black Nose Dace, an effective imitation but also an excellent searching pattern.

| 1 | 2 | 3 |
| 4 | 5 | 6 |

1	Black Nose Dace	
	ART FLICK	
Hook	6X long, sizes 6, **8**, **10**, 12	
Thread	Black 3/0 or 6/0	
Tail	Red wool yarn	
Body	Silver tinsel	
Underwing	White bucktail	
Midwing	Black bear hair or black bucktail	
Overwing	Brown bucktail	

2	Royal Coachman Bucktail	
Hook	6X long, sizes 6, **8**, **10**, 12	
Thread	Black 3/0 or 6/0	
Tail	Golden pheasant tippets	
Body	Peacock herl, red floss, peacock herl	
Hackle	Brown	
Wing	White bucktail	

3	Little Rainbow Trout	
	S. R. SLAYMAKER II	
Hook	6X long, sizes 4, **6**, **8**, 10	
Thread	Black 3/0 or 6/0	
Tail	Green bucktail	
Rib	Oval silver tinsel	
Body	Pink fur dubbing	
Throat	Pink hackle	
Wing	White, pink, and green bucktail	
Topping	Badger hair or gray squirrel tail	
Cheeks	Jungle cock or imitation	

4	Little Brook Trout	
	S. R. SLAYMAKER II	
Hook	6X long, sizes 4, **6**, **8**, 10	
Thread	Black 3/0 or 6/0	
Tail	Green bucktail over red floss	
Rib	Oval silver tinsel	
Body	Cream fur dubbing	
Throat	Orange hackle	
Wing	White, orange, and green bucktail	
Topping	Badger hair or gray squirrel tail	
Cheeks	Jungle cock or imitation	

5	Light Spruce	
Hook	4X or 6X long, sizes 4, 6, **8**, **10**, 12	
Thread	Black 3/0 or 6/0	
Tail	Peacock sword fibers	
Body	Red floss, peacock herl	
Hackle	Silver badger	
Wings	Silver badger hackle feathers	

6	Dark Spruce	
Hook	4X or 6X long, sizes 4, 6, **8**, **10**, 12	
Thread	Black 3/0 or 6/0	
Tail	Peacock sword fibers	
Body	Red floss, peacock herl	
Hackle	Furnace	
Wings	Furnace hackle feathers	

Fishing Notes

Streamers should never be neglected when the water is high, cold, and cloudy, but I use them more often when trout are shallow but not feeding actively on insects. Rig to fish streamers shallow with floating or sinking-tip lines, or deep with sinking lines.

Streamers are especially effective fished across tailouts of pools, in low light, when big trout rise up out of the depths and back down to hang and feed in water that almost exposes their dorsal fins. Get into position upstream and at the edge of the tailout. Cast clear across it. Let the fly swim down to where the water shelves up, then bump it right through the shallows. Watch for V-wakes, but discipline yourself not to set the hook until you feel the fish. Hold on.

Small bucktail and featherwing streamers are perfect for coaxing trout from pools and shallows of small and medium-sized streams.

WOOLLY BUGGERS AND MARABOU LEECHES

Woolly Buggers add the action of marabou to the old and effective Woolly Worm. Though they're near the back of this book, they deserve a prime spot in any list of essential trout flies. If you ever explore new waters or set out fishing without knowing precisely what you'll encounter, you need to be armed with Woolly Buggers in a couple of colors. They'll take trout in a vast array of stillwater and stream situations.

They're most imitative of leeches, but Woolly Buggers also look like pollywogs and dragonfly and damselfly nymphs. If I arrive at a piece of water I've never fished, nearly anywhere in the world, and am in doubt about what to use, I usually begin with an Olive Woolly Bugger and try a black one next.

Woolly Buggers often work as well for steelhead, salmon, and both smallmouth and largemouth bass. The same can be said for simple Marabou Leeches. They look like lots of things that trout eat, though they're tied and fished most often as imitations of leeches in lakes and ponds. I'll list abbreviated steps in tying both Woolly Buggers and Marabou Leeches.

Olive Woolly Bugger	
Hook	3X long, sizes 6, **8, 10,** 12
Weight	15 to 25 turns of lead wire
Thread	Olive 3/0 or 6/0
Tail	Olive marabou and olive Krystal Flash
Body	Olive chenille
Hackle	Brown hen or rooster

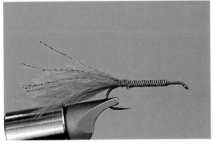

WOOLLY BUGGER

Step 1. Debarb the hook, fix it in the vise, and weight it with fifteen to twenty-five turns of lead wire the diameter of the hook shank. I rarely underweight Woolly Buggers. Layer thread over the hook shank, and secure the lead. Strip or clip a thick patch of marabou from a feather. Use more than you think you need; it compresses when wet. Measure it the length of the hook, and tie it in at the bend. Clip the excess butts. Measure six to ten strands of Krystal Flash the length of the tail, and tie it in.

Step 2. Clip several inches of chenille from the skein. Strip $1/8$ inch of the fibers from the core strands. Tie this in at the base of the tail. Select a hen or poor-grade rooster hackle with fibers two to two and a half hook gaps long. Hold it by the tip, and run your thumb and forefinger along the stem to flare the fibers. Tie in the hackle by the tip, over the gathered tip fibers rather than the exposed hackle stem. If you make your tie-in over the fragile stem, the thread will often break the stem when you begin to wind it.

Step 3. Take the first turn of body chenille behind the hackle, the rest forward to the hook eye. Tie it off and clip the excess. Use your hackle pliers to take evenly spaced turns of hackle forward to the end of the body. Take an extra turn there if you have hackle left. Tie it off and clip the stem. You can finish the fly as it is. I recommend working thread turns back through the hackle and forward again to the front. This locks the hackle in and protects it from the teeth of trout.

BLACK MARABOU LEECH

Step 1. Debarb the hook and fix it in the vise. Weight the hook with standard lead wire. Layer thread over the shank and lead wraps. Strip or clip a substantial amount of marabou from a feather. Measure it the length of the hook shank, and tie it in at the bend of the hook. Clip the excess butts. Dub fur forward to the midpoint of the hook shank.

Step 2. Clip or strip an amount of marabou equal to the tail. Measure it the length of the hook, and tie it in at the midpoint of the hook. Clip the excess butts. Dub fur forward to a point three or four hook-eye lengths behind the eye.

Step 3. Clip or strip a third segment of marabou equal to the tail and first wing. Measure it the length of the hook, and tie it in at the end of the body. Clip the excess butts. Dub a short fur head in front of this last wing. Form a neat thread head, whip-finish once or twice, clip the thread, and cement the head.

Useful Variations

Most leeches are black, dark olive, or reddish brown. The last are called blood leeches. Flies tied to match them sometimes use red or purple marabou, which is an alternative not listed here but that you should keep in mind. The Brown Woolly Bugger fishes for them most of the time.

By far the most useful Woolly Buggers, and also Marabou Leeches, are the black and olive versions. All Woolly Bugger and Marabou Leech dressings can be altered with the addition of beadheads behind the eye. The jury is out on which is more effective—with or without beads.

My most common damselfly nymph imitation is a size 10 or 12 Olive Woolly Bugger with the tail and hackle thinned to wisps. When dragonfly nymphs are present and trout are taking them, I truncate a size 6 or 8 Olive Woolly Bugger by pinching off the back half of its tails. The fly is then an adequate imitation of the portly early stage of that dashing aerial predator.

1	2	3
4	5	6

1	Black Woolly Bugger
Hook	3X long, sizes 6, **8, 10,** 12
Weight	15 to 25 turns of lead wire
Thread	Black 3/0 or 6/0
Tail	Black marabou and black Krystal Flash
Body	Black chenille
Hackle	Black hen or rooster

2	Brown Woolly Bugger
Hook	3X long, sizes 6, **8, 10,** 12
Weight	15 to 25 turns of lead wire
Thread	Brown 3/0 or 6/0
Tail	Brown marabou and red Krystal Flash
Body	Brown chenille
Hackle	Brown hen or rooster

3	Olive & Black Woolly Bugger
Hook	3X long, sizes 6, **8, 10,** 12
Weight	15 to 25 turns of lead wire
Thread	Black 3/0 or 6/0
Tail	Olive marabou and olive Krystal Flash
Body	Olive chenille
Hackle	Black hen or rooster

4	Black Marabou Leech
Hook	6X long, sizes 4, **6, 8,** 10
Weight	15 to 25 turns of lead wire
Thread	Black 3/0 or 6/0
Tail	Black marabou
Body	Black fur dubbing
Wings	Black marabou

5	Olive Marabou Leech
Hook	6X long, sizes 4, **6, 8,** 10
Weight	15 to 25 turns of lead wire
Thread	Olive 3/0 or 6/0
Tail	Olive marabou
Body	Olive fur dubbing
Wings	Olive marabou

6	Blood Marabou Leech
Hook	6X long, sizes 4, **6, 8,** 10
Weight	15 to 25 turns of lead wire
Thread	Red 3/0 or 6/0
Tail	Red marabou
Body	Red fur dubbing
Wings	Red marabou

Fishing Notes

The inherent action of marabou is often all the movement you need to attract trout. If you're fishing a stillwater and trout are deep, use a sinking line and count the fly down to the depth you want. Leech imitations seem especially effective when sent down deep in marl-darkened lakes. Cast out and let the line take the fly down slowly. That's the part of the retrieve when you'll get most takes: when there is no retrieve at all. Watch your line tip carefully where it enters the water. If it moves, set the hook.

After you've let the fly get down, bring it back with a creeping hand-twist retrieve, as slow as you can discipline yourself to go. If you feel a tap, drop your rod tip, wait a beat or two, then pick it up gently again. A trout has tried to inhale the fly, which failed to back into its mouth because it's tethered to your leader. The surprised trout will swing around to try again. If you drop the rod, hesitate, then lift it again, the fly will often be right where you want it: lodged in the trout's mouth.

I often cast leech dressings long in lakes, let them sink a foot or two on a wet-tip line, then retrieve them as fast as I can. My theory is that when a leech senses a trout on its tail, it takes off as fast as it can swim. Trout take off after it when they see it and hit with a whack. The theory is not proven, but the method is successful.

Marabou streamers are deadly when cast off points, over the shallows, and beyond drop-offs in lakes and ponds.

MATUKAS AND ZONKERS

The Matuka is a streamer style that came out of New Zealand and became quite popular on our own continent, primarily because these streamers look like natural baitfish and fool lots of trout. Matukas are also easy to tie, which means you can fish them down on the bottom and around the kinds of woody cover that hold large fish, without worrying about the tying time you'll sacrifice if you hang up and lose one.

As with most streamers, Matukas are usually tied in the largest sizes, 2, 4, and 6; my advice, however, is to try them on the smaller side, say sizes 8 and 10. It's true that big fish take big flies, but it's just as true that they'll take smaller ones as well, and sometimes less reluctantly.

Zonkers, designed by Dan Byford, are flashy flies designed to represent big bites and to be sent deep after large trout. I recommend that you tie at least a few of them in sizes 2 and 4 and keep them handy for those moments when you want to probe the darkest depths of a pool or a long, deep run and would like to catch the largest trout that lurks down there.

Black Matuka

Hook	3X or 4X long, sizes 4, 6, **8, 10,** 12
Weight	20 to 30 turns of lead wire
Thread	Black 3/0 or 6/0
Rib	Copper wire
Body	Black chenille
Gills	Red wool yarn
Wing	Black hen
Hackle	Black hen

MATUKA

Step 1. Debarb the hook and fix it in the vise. Weight the hook with lead wire the diameter of the shank. I recommend you weight your Matukas heavily. Tie in several inches of ribbing wire at the bend of the hook. Clip the excess at the back of the lead weighting wraps to form an even underbody. Strip 1/8 inch of chenille from the core threads, and tie in the chenille at the bend of the hook.

Step 2. Wind the chenille to a point about one-fifth to one-fourth the length of the shank behind the eye. Tie it off and clip the excess. Tie in red wool yarn, and take two or three wraps of it at the end of the body. Select four matched hen feathers twice the length of the hook, using two feathers from each side of a neck or saddle patch so their curves complement each other. Pair the feathers, and meld them so their concave sides are together. Measure them one hook length beyond the bend, and tie them in at the head of the fly.

Step 3. Hold the wing down on top of the hook bend with your off hand, and form a gap in the top fibers with your tying hand. Take two turns of ribbing wire through this gap, securing the wing to the hook shank at the end of the body. Move forward 1/8 to 1/4 inch, depending on the hook size, form another gap, and take a turn of ribbing wire though it. Repeat this process with evenly spaced ribbing wraps to the hook eye, securing the wing to the top of the hook. Tie off the ribbing and cut or break off the excess.

Step 4. Select a hackle feather from the same neck you used for the wings. It should have fibers two to two and a half times the hook gap. Strip fuzzy fibers from the stem, tie in the feather with its concave side toward the hook shank, and take four to five hackle wraps just behind the hook eye. Tie off and clip the excess, form a neat thread head, whip-finish, and clip the thread. Cement the head with a couple of coats, and the fly is finished.

ZONKER

Step 1. Weight the hook, and start red thread at the bend. Unravel 1/4 to 1/2 inch of mylar piping, slip it over the hook, and tie it off just ahead of the unraveled strands. Stretch the piping past the hook eye, and cut the excess just beyond it. Push it back, start black thread, and tie off the piping two or three hook-eye lengths behind the eye. Measure a bunch of hen grizzly hackle fibers half the hook length, and tie them in on the underside of the body as a throat.

Step 2. Cut a rabbit strip from the hide about half the width of the hook gap, or use a precut Zonker strip. Measure the strip twice the length of the hook, and tie it in at the head. Form a neat thread head, whip-finish twice, clip the thread, and cement the head well. Open a gap in the fur just above the hook bend. Use several turns of red thread through this gap to fix the fur strip to the hook. Use two whip finishes to secure the red thread. Clip the thread and cement this tie-down point just as you did for the head.

Useful Variations

Black and olive seem to be the most useful colors in both the Matuka and Zonker styles. They are, however, tied in nearly every color of the rainbow for which you can find dyed Matuka patches and Zonker strips. The best Matuka feathers I've found are from the rooster breast patches marketed under the brand name Chickabou.

Matukas and Zonkers can be tied in any colors for which you have suitable materials. If you're sticking with an essential list of flies for placement in a limited set of fly boxes, I recommend the Olive Matuka and Black Matuka.

The Zonker, especially, finds its applications far from limited to trout. It is excellent for both species of bass and for untold species of saltwater fish. If you expand your fishing and go after those, purchase Zonker strips in white, red, yellow, and purple and tie Zonkers in those colors.

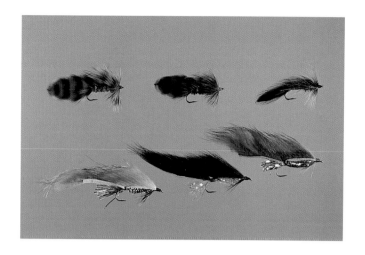

1	2	3
4	5	6

1	Olive Matuka
Hook	3X or 4X long, sizes 4, 6, **8**, **10**, 12
Weight	20 to 30 turns of lead wire
Thread	Olive 3/0 or 6/0
Rib	Copper wire
Body	Olive chenille
Gills	Red wool yarn
Wing	Olive dyed grizzly hen
Hackle	Olive dyed grizzly hen

2	Brown Matuka
Hook	3X or 4X long, sizes 4, 6, **8**, **10**, 12
Weight	20 to 30 turns of lead wire
Thread	Brown 3/0 or 6/0
Rib	Copper wire
Body	Brown chenille
Gills	Red wool yarn
Wing	Brown dyed grizzly hen
Hackle	Brown dyed grizzly hen

3	Spruce Matuka
Hook	3X or 4X long, sizes 4, 6, **8**, **10**, 12
Weight	20 to 30 turns of lead wire
Thread	Black 3/0 or 6/0
Rib	Copper wire
Body	Red floss and peacock herl
Wing	Furnace hen
Hackle	Furnace hen

4	Zonker
	DAN BYFORD
Hook	6X long, sizes **2**, **4**, 6, 8, 10
Thread	Black and red 3/0 or 6/0
Tail and body	Silver mylar piping
Hackle	Grizzly hen
Wing	Natural rabbit fur strip or precut Zonker strip

5	Black Zonker
	DAN BYFORD
Hook	6X long, sizes **2**, **4**, 6, 8, 10
Thread	Black and red 3/0 or 6/0
Tail and body	Pearl mylar piping
Hackle	Black hen
Wing	Black rabbit fur strip

6	Olive Zonker
	DAN BYFORD
Hook	6X long, sizes **2**, **4**, 6, 8, 10
Thread	Olive and red 3/0 or 6/0
Tail and body	Gold mylar piping
Hackle	Olive dyed grizzly hen
Wing	Olive rabbit fur strip

Fishing Notes

The primary purpose of both Matukas and Zonkers is to entice large trout—those that have attained enough size to feed on baitfish. You can fish Matukas or Zonkers with a floating line in the shallows along the banks or across the tailouts of pools. Retrieve with staccato strips. The bank method is often effective when employed from a moving boat. As you drift along, place the fly close to the bank, give it a few seconds to sink, then retrieve it away for a few feet. If nothing happens, lift the fly and cast to the next bit of bank. Probe with a few extra casts around any boulders, logs, or other cover. To fish tailouts, coax the fly to swim across the shallow water as you approach it and pass it in a boat. Better yet, get out and wade to fish them more carefully.

When probing deep sanctuary water, switch to a wet-tip or full-sinking line. Give the fly plenty of time to sink, and retrieve it slowly. Give a big trout a good look at the fly, time to think about it. You'll have to coax it with your Matuka or Zonker.

Weighted Matukas and Zonkers cannot be beaten for prying the largest trout out of the deepest pools in any stream or river.

CONCLUSION

Your purpose in working with *Essential Trout Flies* is not to tie all the flies listed, but to select carefully and fill two to four boxes with flies that will take trout for you at most times, in most places. Those fly boxes should contain flies that cover the repeated color themes of natural trout food forms. They should also cover the shapes and sizes of those various forms. That's why you choose a full box of dry flies, a wide array of nymphs, plus a few central wet flies and streamers.

Your boxes should be filled for the most part with flies that resemble more than a single insect or other food form. For example, the Parachute Adams is at once an excellent searching dry fly and also a fair imitation of many mayfly hatches. The Muddler Minnow is a sculpin imitation but can be floated for a grasshopper or retrieved out from the bank as a chub or other baitfish pattern.

Some of the flies in your boxes should be tied for specific hatches that you encounter often and must match to fool many trout. For example, the Olive Hairwing Dun is specific for little olive mayflies *(Baetis),* in sizes 18 and 20. It needs to be in the box because that hatch happens throughout the United States, in Great Britain, down in Chile and Argentina, and in New Zealand.

You need flies that fish for many things, and you need flies that fish for ubiquitous things. You also need flies for things that your waters serve up to trout often and in abundance. You need to find a style in this book that matches their form, and then tie a size and color variation for the species over which you're fishing. All tying begins with pattern styles. The variations you work on them can be the standards I've listed or your own response to the trout foods that you collect, based upon the standards.

Each fly that you tie, and drop into the boxes out of which you fish most often, should be one in which you have great confidence. That confidence can come because the fly has a long history of catching trout, such as the Royal Wulff. It can also come because you've tried the fly yourself and caught lots of trout on it when you weren't doing much with anything else. That's why Dave

Whitlock's Fox Squirrel in size 14 or 16 is usually the first nymph I tie on, if nothing leads me in another direction. The first time I used it, I abruptly caught several nice trout in a row, in water where I hadn't been catching a thing. That fly won my confidence and has worked ever since.

The following flies have become the core that I carry in my own two essential boxes—the flies in the boxes constantly in my Sidekick II belt bag or the main pockets of my vest, wherever I go in the world of trout:

Adams 14, 16
Olive Hairwing Dun 16, 18, 20
Pale Morning Sparkle Dun 16, 18
Royal Wulff 12, 14
Parachute Adams 14, 16
Elk Hair Caddis 12, 14, 16
Deer Hair Caddis 12, 14, 16
Stimulator 6, 8, 10
Adams Midge 18, 20
Griffith's Gnat 18, 20
Parachute Hopper, 10,12
Gold-Ribbed Hare's Ear 12, 14
Fox Squirrel 14, 16
Pheasant Tail 16, 18, 20
Olive Beadhead 12, 14, 16
Olive Scud 12, 14
Brooks Stone 6, 8, 10
Partridge & Yellow 12, 14
Starling & Herl 16
March Brown Flymph 12, 14
Leadwing Coachman 12, 14
Muddler Minnow 6, 8, 10
Black Marabou Muddler 6, 8, 10
Olive Woolly Bugger 8, 10, 12
Black Woolly Bugger 8, 10, 12

This is my list of essential trout flies—my list within the list. Yours should be different, based on where you live, the waters, and the way you prefer to fish. If you start with these, though, you won't find many situations in which you lack a fly that will catch trout.

INDEX OF PATTERNS

ABOUT THE AUTHOR

Dave Hughes began fly-fishing for trout in his early teens. For the last twenty years, he has made a study of trout streams and lakes, the natural foods on which trout feed, and the flies that take trout in the widest variety of circumstances.

Dave has fly-fished for trout across the United States and Canada, as well as in Chile, Argentina, and New Zealand. He is founding president of Oregon Trout, was awarded life membership in the Federation of Fly Fishers, and in 1992 was presented the Vernon S. "Pete" Hidy life membership award by the Flyfisher's Club of Oregon for his contributions to angling literature.

Dave's articles, essays, and fiction have appeared in *Fly Fisherman, Fly Rod & Reel, Flyfishing, American Angler, Field & Stream,* and *Gray's Sporting Journal.* He lives in Portland, Oregon, with his wife, Masako Tani, and daughter, Kosumo.

BOOKS BY DAVE HUGHES

Western Hatches (with Rick Hafele)
An Angler's Astoria
American Fly Tying Manual
Handbook of Hatches
Reading the Water
Tackle & Technique
Tactics for Trout
Strategies for Stillwater
Dry Fly Fishing
Nymph Fishing
Fly Fishing Basics
Deschutes: River of Renewal
The Yellowstone River and Its Angling
Big Indian Creek
Wet Flies
Western Streamside Guide
Trout Flies

Dave Hughes

JIM SCHOLLMEYER